MW01130322

THE COMPLETE GUIDE TO SIAMESE CATS

Candace Darnforth

LP Media Inc. Publishing
Text copyright © 2022 by LP Media Inc.
All rights reserved.

No part of this book may be reproduced or transmitted in any form or by any means, electronic or mechanical, including photocopying, recording, or by an information storage and retrieval system – except by a reviewer who may quote brief passages in a review to be printed in a magazine or newspaper – without permission in writing from the publisher.
For information address LP Media Inc. Publishing, 3178 253rd Ave. NW, Isanti, MN 55040

www.lpmedia.org

Publication Data

Candace Darnforth

The Complete Guide to Siamese Cats – First edition.

Summary: "Successfully raising a Siamese Cat from kitten to old age" – Provided by publisher.

ISBN: 978-1-954288-53-9

[1. Siamese Cats – Non-Fiction] I. Title.

This book has been written with the published intent to provide accurate and authoritative information in regard to the subject matter included. While every reasonable precaution has been taken in preparation of this book the author and publisher expressly disclaim responsibility for any errors, omissions, or adverse effects arising from the use or application of the information contained inside. The techniques and suggestions are to be used at the reader's discretion and are not to be considered a substitute for professional veterinary care. If you suspect a medical problem with your cat, consult your veterinarian.

Design by Sorin Rădulescu
First hardcover edition, 2022

TABLE OF CONTENTS

INTRODUCTION

Welcome, and thank you for making a commitment to learning more about your Siamese cat. Whether you are a first-time cat owner or have had cats your entire life, this book will help you gain a deeper appreciation and understanding of why your cat does what she does and how you can manage her behavior.

Looking for a snuggle buddy? Then look no further, as a Siamese cat will not disappoint —they are a people-loving breed that forms a very tight bond with their humans. A prominent characteristic of this breed is following their owners around the house and keenly being interested in whatever you are doing.

Siamese cats are one of the most beloved cat breeds in North America, and for good reason — they are extremely affectionate, intelligent, and elegant creatures. Siamese cats are one of the most recognized of all companion breeds due to their sleek, distinctive appearance.

Photo Courtesy of Karina Dunbar

Contrary to popular belief, this sophisticated-looking breed's fame did not begin with Disney's mischievous felines humming the tune "We are Siamese if you please." In real life, they are much more pleasant than these iconic Disney notorious rascals. The history of the Siamese cat dates back to around the 14th century, making them one of the oldest domesticated breeds in the world.

Siamese cats have a strong desire to interact with someone, enjoying the company of other cats, children, and even strangers. However, their affectionate disposition makes them prone to separation anxiety or depression if left alone too long.

The highly inquisitive Siamese have a playful, puppy-like personality, and can be easily taught to play fetch, give high fives, and even walk on a leash. Despite their elegant looks, Siamese cats make dynamic pets, best-suited for attentive and loving owners. If that sounds like you, then you are in for a treat with one of the most loyal and playful companions in the world.

CHAPTER 1

Meet the Siamese Cat

Siamese cats are probably best known for their sleek, distinctive appearance. Even though the majority of Siamese have silver-gray fur with piercing blue eyes, these attractive felines' coats can also be brown, cream, and lilac, among other coat variations. However, there is so much more to the Siamese cat than their mysteriously good looks.

What is a Siamese Cat?

Siamese cats may look regal and elegant, but there is not an ounce of snobbery in this breed. Siamese cats are one of the world's most affectionate and loyal cats. Human attention is the one thing this breed cannot get enough of. All Siamese cats are extremely fond of their people.

This breed is highly intelligent, agile, athletic, and loves to play. They are also very opinionated and talkative. They are not shy and will tell you exactly what they are thinking in their loud raspy voices, and they will expect you to pay attention and act upon their advice.

Siamese cats are also very helpful and will follow you around the house, often supervising you while you perform your household chores. When it is time to sit down and enjoy a cup of tea or watch television, your Siamese will be snuggled up on your lap, and at night, she will most likely be in bed with you, probably under the covers. Perhaps that is why Siamese cats are often called Velcro cats.

With their affectionate, friendly, and chatty personalities, it is easy to see why Siamese cats are one of the five most popular breeds in North America.

History of the Siamese Cat

Siamese cats are one of the oldest domesticated cats in the world. History indicates that the breed originated in Thailand (formally known as Siam) in the early 14th century when they first appeared in a Thai manuscript.

Photo Courtesy of Becky Brown

In Siam (Thailand), these mystical, stunning cats were exclusive for the royal family and the upper-class residents. It was a great honor to own Siamese cats, and theft of one was punishable by death. Also, it was believed that the Siamese cats guarded the hundreds of sacred Buddhist temples in Siam.

In Siam, when a royal family member died, it was believed their soul would be reincarnated in a Siamese cat. For this reason, the Siamese cats would spend their days being pampered in a temple with doting monks.

In the past, Siamese cats had genetic defects, such as a hooked tail and crossed eyes. Fortunately, breeders have almost been able to completely eliminate these unwanted traits. Unfortunately, if a Siamese cat is born with a kinked tail or crossed eyes, it will be disqualified from participating at The International Cat Association (TICA) shows.

According to an old Siam legend, these genetic mutations were due to a Siamese cat who had the task of guarding a precious goblet. This Siamese cat was extremely dedicated to his job and hooked his tail around the vase to prevent it from falling, staring at it intently for hours at a time. This left the Siamese cat with a permanently hooked tail and crossed eyes.

Another legend states that the temple cats were valued by the king not only for their exquisite beauty but their abilities to protect the king and his family. The legend states that the king had the Siamese cats perched on tall columns around the throne as guard cats. According to the legend, if anyone threatened the king, the cats would pounce on the individual. Due to their size and the strength the Siamese would be able to knock the person to the ground, often scratching their face.

It is believed the first Siamese cats were exported to Europe in the late 1800s when Siam's King Chulalongkorn sent several Siamese cats to Europe as emissaries for his kingdom. A British consul named Mr. Owen Gould returned to Britain with a pair of Siamese cats for his sister — Mrs. Veley. Shortly after, Mrs. Veley co-founded the first Siamese Cat Club in Europe.

The Siamese's striking good looks were not always appreciated. For example, at a renowned Crystal Palace Cat Show in London in 1871, one journalist described the Siamese breed as "an unnatural, nightmare kind of cat." Thankfully, that untruthful description has been long forgotten, and the breed now draws admirers wherever it goes.

Even though Siamese cats were domesticated companions in Asia for centuries, they did not make their debut in the United States until the 19th century. Apparently, Siamese cats do not only have a history of gracing the royal courts in Siam but also in the White House.

Photo Courtesy of Crystal Miller

A U.S. diplomat serving in Thailand gifted the U.S. President Rutherford B. Hayes' wife a Siamese cat named Siam.

President Jimmy Carter's daughter Amy Lynn Carter also had a beloved Siamese cat named Misty, who lived in the White House during Carter's presidency.

For many years, in the western hemisphere, Siamese cats were referred to as the Royal Cats of Siam or the Temple Cats. But over time, the breed's name was shortened to Siamese in honor of the country they represented.

In 1955, a sinister pair of Siamese cats named Si and Am caused mischief in the hit film *Lady and the Tramp*. The twin Siamese cats got a cocker spaniel blamed for all of the havoc they wreaked in the movie. In 1963, a Siamese cat named Tao starred in another Disney movie called The *Incredible Journey*. The film follows the adventures of two dogs and a Siamese cat who find their way back home.

Back in the early 1960, two Siamese cats were living in the Dutch embassy in Moscow and began scratching incessantly at a wall. The ambassador suspected his cats could hear a noise that could not be detected by the human ear. His assumption was correct – there were thirty small microphones concealed behind the wall.

Shortly after these Siamese cats foiled this attempted Russian espionage, Walt Disney produced a movie called That Darn Cat starring a Siamese cat who prevents a kidnapping.

Physical Appearance

Siamese cats are best known for their distinctive appearance and striking, almond-shaped eyes.

Siamese cats are a medium-sized breed, often weighing between eight to twelve pounds when fully grown. Growing to a length of fifteen to twenty inches, not including the tail. They have sleek, muscular bodies with long legs, making them great jumpers. Siamese cats love to perch on shelves or cat trees to observe their surroundings.

Your Siamese cat's diet and nutrition should be strictly controlled, as her legs are not designed to hold up the extra weight. This breed will quickly show weight gain; often, a pot belly will be noticed after a day of overindulging.

Siamese cats have short, non-shedding coats that do not require a ton of grooming. As such, Siamese cats can be a good fit for allergy sufferers. However, these cats love to be brushed and often will interpret it as a moment of being pampered.

As we mentioned in the introduction of this chapter, Siamese cats can have a range of coat colors; however, their coat color isn't entirely determined by genetics. Unlike other cat breeds, Siamese cats have a special modifier gene that prevents pigment from developing in their fur, resulting

Photo Courtesy of Celine Guilbaud

Photo Courtesy of Susie Kelley

in albinism. However, for some unknown reason, this gene only affects their fur above 102.5 degrees.

When the Siamese cat's body temperature drops below 100 degrees — or the feline is exposed to a colder environment — genes for her coat turn on and carry pigment to her fur.

It is not unusual for Siamese cats to be born completely white and to develop their markings in the following weeks. The womb provides a warm, controlled temperature, which blocks the activation of the feline's color gene. After birth, the kitten is exposed to cooler temperatures, resulting in the kitten starting to develop pigmentation around its face, paws, and tail. Because the cat's body is cooler around the extremities, the pigment is more heavily deposited there.

Behavioral Characteristics

The affectionate Siamese will dedicate herself completely to her new family, but she requires them to be as dedicated to her as she is to them. Often, Siamese cats are dubbed "Velcro kitties" because their love for their family is so intense. This breed will stick by your side, following you in the pursuit of extra snuggles and attention.

Siamese cats thrive on positive human interaction. They are deeply sensitive and will take any harsh words personally. Be sure to use positive reinforcement while training your cat to use the litter box or teaching him your sofa is not a scratching toy. Later on in this book, we will discuss how to use positive reinforcement while training your cat.

Siamese cats love to snuggle and be held. They do need their own space occasionally, but often that means hanging out a few feet from you instead of right on top of you. Do not be surprised if your Siamese dubs one person in your household as her person and forms a tighter bond with that individual. But this affectionate breed will still cuddle up to everyone in the family.

This attractive breed is one of the most intelligent cats around. Siamese cats can be trained to do tricks and even walk on a leash. But do not be fooled; like most intelligent beings, you will discover your Siamese has her own personality and desires, so she cannot be trained to do everything you might wish.

You will need to keep your cat's active brain busy with puzzle toys and a big cat tree for her to climb and explore. Never leave your Siamese cat home alone without some form of entertainment; otherwise, you will come home to a very upset little cat.

If you already have a Siamese cat or have spent time around one, then you already know that they are extremely talkative. They are not shy about vocalizing their opinions about their food or any interesting observations about whatever they encounter throughout the day.

This breed makes a distinctive sound that most felines are unable to make. For this reason, Siamese cats have earned the nickname "meezer" due to their unique, child-like sounds. Some pet owners attest their fur babies sound like a baby crying or a chirping bird. Due to their chatterbox nature, they will let you know whenever they need something.

This breed is a bundle of energy and requires a lot of mental stimulation and exercise. Even if your cat has a truck-load of crinkly toys to play with, she will not enjoy being left to her own devices for too long. Siamese cats thrive in a home where people spend most of their time with them, and if left alone for long periods, they can become anxious and depressed.

Besides being emotionally sensitive, Siamese cats are also sensitive to physical elements, such as the cold. Make sure to provide your cat with plenty of cuddles, a warm blanket, and maybe even a little sweater during the colder winter months.

Photo Courtesy of Isabelle Hamers

Age Expectancy

A typical Siamese cat's life span is approximately twelve to twenty years. Your cat will be a senior around twelve years of age. Siamese cats are prone to dental and some respiratory conditions, but other than that, the breed has no significant health conditions.

Quality nutrition, adequate exercise, and regular veterinarian checks will maximize your cat's life expectancy. Since the feline's diet is such an important factor for longevity, choose a high-quality cat food from day one. In Chapter Ten of this book, you will find detailed information to help you decipher cat food labels, find the best sources of protein for your cat, and more.

According to experts, the number one factor in all long-lived cats is remaining indoors. Felines who are allowed to roam freely outside are more likely to get in cat fights, be hit by a car, and catch unwanted diseases and parasites. Domestic cats that are allowed regularly outside have an average life span of two to seven years.

Read on to get more information about whether you should let your cat explore the great outdoors or not.

Indoor or Outdoor

Should you let your Siamese roam? Is it safe for your cat to venture outdoors?

All cats, regardless of their breed, yearn for the great outdoors and often rush to the front door every time they hear it creak open, or they sit staring out the window, longing to go outside. Without a doubt, all cats love to roam, but is it safe?

Generally, cats that are allowed to roam outside are less likely to develop behavioral issues, such as urinating outside of the litter box, mounting, or stalking and attacking people inside of your house. Also, cats who frequently go outside are less likely to scratch furniture, as they are already clawing at trees outside. However, these behavioral issues can be easily remedied by providing your indoor cat with stimulation and creating an environment your feline will enjoy.

Siamese cats need to climb, jump, scratch, hide, and run. Keep your Siamese cat busy indoors with a scratching post, cat tower with hiding holes, and squeaky toys. Siamese cats are extremely curious and love to watch what is happening outside. Encourage your cat to spy on the neighbors by creating a window seat or perch. If possible, place a bird feeder outside the window to keep your fur baby entertained for hours.

Indoor cats are less active than outdoor cats, which increases their risk of developing diabetes, arthritis, obesity, and heart disease. But there are much greater health risks for cats who spend a significant amount of time outside. Being exposed to the elements and having contact with other animals creates a completely different set of problems, including:

- Hypothermia or heatstroke
- Fungal, bacterial, and viral infections
- Contagious diseases, such as feline immunodeficiency virus (FIV), feline leukemia, and rabies
- Wounds from fighting with other cats or animals
- Trauma from being abused by people or hit by a car
- Parasites such as roundworms, ringworm, and fleas
- Poisoning from consuming toxic chemicals, such as rat poison or antifreeze

Experts agree that keeping your cat indoors is the healthier choice. But if you want to give your Siamese the best of both worlds, you can train your cat to walk on a leash. There are specially designed cat harnesses that will keep your Siamese cat safe. Or you can use a portable cat pen — an enclosed area that lets your cat get fresh air without being completely free.

Siamese cats have been human companions for thousands of years and are not very street smart. Experts do not recommend allowing your Siamese to roam about unsupervised. Before making a decision to let your cat go outside, be sure to weigh the advantages and disadvantages and talk to your veterinarian.

HELPFUL TIP

National Siamese Cat Club (NSCC)

The National Siamese Cat Club (NSCC) is a Cat Fanciers Association (CFA) breed club. The NSCC was founded in 1946 and produces an annual all-breed cat show. This organization advocates for the breed and promotes breeding Siamese cats according to the CFA standards. For more information, visit www.nationalsiamese.com.

Is a Siamese Cat the Right Fit for You?

> "*In my experience, I have found that this beautiful breed thrives best in active homes. They want to play and move, while at the same time being ready to snuggle at any moment. They love being part of the family and being part of the everlasting moments we as humans hold dear to our hearts. They love talking and even arguing with their people about what they want to do and what they know they can't do. I always tell my 'soon to be extended family' that owning this breed of cat is just like adopting a child. When they add a Siamese cat into the family, they are going to have to include the cat on family trips, even if it's just going on a walk.*"
>
> AMANDA WILLIAMS
> *AW Cattery*

Siamese cats are exceptional companions — but they need companionship in return. For this reason, Siamese cats are best suited for households where someone is home most of the time, which may include human family members, the family dog, or another cat, such as a Siamese.

Do not get a Siamese cat if you do not like the idea of having a chatty busybody. On the other hand, if you enjoy having someone to chit-chat with throughout the day, then a Siamese is for you.

Often, Siamese cats are described as having a dog-personality, without the high maintenance of having a canine. This breed is extremely intelligent and can quickly learn to play fetch, open drawers, or even walk on a leash.

Have children or other pets? Siamese cats have a good tolerance for children, as long as the children are taught how to interact with kittens and cats. All it takes is one bad experience, and your Siamese will be terrified of little children for the rest of his life. Siamese love animals and generally get along with dogs and cats.

No time for grooming — No problem. Siamese cats require little grooming and, like most shorthair breeds, pride themselves in caring for themselves. Siamese cats only need a light brushing once a week to keep them looking in tip-top shape.

Another factor to take into consideration is Siamese cats thrive in a stable, predictable environment and get visibly upset by any changes to their routine or environment. In other words, Siamese cats generally do not make good travel companions.

- If you already have pets, please consider the following before making the decision to add a Siamese cat to your household:
- Is your home large enough for all of the pets to have adequate space and territory to call their own?
- Are there any current pets suffering from chronic illnesses, so the added stress of a new cat may worsen the health issues?

Are there any pets suffering from behavioral issues such as separation anxiety or inappropriate marking?

Siamese cats are ideal pets — you will never get tired of looking at their regal appearance, and they will do everything in their power to become fully involved in your family life. However, this need for attention means the breed suffers when left alone for long periods of time, so they are not ideal pets for an empty house that is void of people or other pets.

CHAPTER 2

Choosing a Siamese Cat

> *I have had people come visit a litter of kittens to pick one out for their family. A kitten will often pick you! One time I had a woman who visited my cattery to choose a kitten; she wanted a little chocolate point kitten. Well, a little lilac point kitten decided this girl was HER PERSON, no 'ifs,' 'ands,' or 'buts.' This little lilac point kitten was all over this lady, would not get off her lap, played with her clothes, and just fell in LOVE! This woman decided to come by again another day to see what would happen; she really wanted that chocolate point. She came by two more times, and the chocolate kitten would not even look her way; in fact, she ran away from her! But that little lilac kitten was all over her again. She decided on the lilac kitten when the time came to take her home. She called me a few months later, telling me it was the best decision she ever made; that little kitten was her soul mate!*
>
> KAREN SPOHN
> *Candi Dasa cattery*

It is easy to be won over by a Siamese cat. They have unique, vibrant personalities and make wonderful companions.

Choosing your new four-pawed best friend should not be taken lightly. There are so many details involved in picking out your kitten. In this chapter, we will discuss everything you need to know about choosing your new best friend.

Purchasing vs. Adopting

Should you buy or adopt your Siamese cat? Most people contemplating getting a cat will ask themselves this question at some point.

There are passionate advocates for both options, but ultimately, it is your decision and your decision alone. Nobody should pressure you into buying or adopting your new four-pawed companion. However, it is helpful to be well-informed about your different options, so you can make the best choice for your personal circumstances.

Photo Courtesy of April Tinnin Sapphire Kittens Cattery

ADOPTING A SHELTER CAT

Adopting a cat from a local shelter or rescue organization can be a most fulfilling experience. You'll never forget that irresistible, pleading "get me out of here face" and the feel-good emotions as you walk out of the shelter with your new cat.

There are many negative stigmas surrounding shelter cats. One is that they will have behavioral issues, or they will be unpredictable. The facts show, though, that the majority of shelter cats are surrendered to the shelter because of a change in the pet owner's circumstances, which have nothing to do with the feline's behavior.

In most cases, you will not be able to meet the shelter cat's parents — so you will not know anything about your Siamese cat's genetic legacy. Also, you will know little to nothing about the cat's life experiences.

PROS AND CONS OF ADOPTING A CAT FROM A LOCAL SHELTER:

The benefits:

- The majority of shelter cats are already neutered/spayed and microchipped.
- You are saving the life of the Siamese that you are adopting and making space in the shelter for another cat in need.
- The shelter will be able to give you a general idea of the cat's personality, so there should be fewer surprises once you bring your cat home.
- Many adult Siamese cats are already potty-trained.
- The love and appreciation from a shelter cat are incomparable!

The costs of adopting can be considerably lower than buying a Siamese cat from a reputable breeder. According to the Animal Humane Society, adoption fees for cats and kittens can run from $120 to $670, depending on the shelter.

The price of a Siamese kitten will vary depending on different factors, such as whether you are looking for a pet Siamese kitten or a show kitten. You can expect to pay more if you buy a cat with breeding rights. Also, there may be variations in price depending on the area where you live. The average price for a pedigree Siamese kitten is $600 to $1000. Beware of Siamese kittens that are priced too good to be true, as they probably are.

The challenges:

- You might not know the cat's family history or where she came from.

- Many shelters have strict requirements for adopting one of their cats to ensure the animal does not end up in a shelter again in the future.
- Since the Siamese is a pedigree breed in the United States, it can be difficult to find one in a local shelter.
- Finding a Siamese kitten in a shelter can almost be impossible, and you may have to adopt an older cat.
- Some cats have been treated cruelly by their previous owners, which has left them with emotional scars and behavior issues.

Photo Courtesy of Annette & Joseph Keawkalaya

Rescues and Shelters 101

Animal shelters throughout the United States are overburdened with millions of abandoned pets each year. By adopting a Siamese cat, you are making room for other cats in need. You are giving your new feline friend a second chance to have a loving home, plus the cost of adoption goes directly toward the shelter so that they can continue to help more cats in need.

Many Siamese are patiently waiting for someone to adopt them and take them to their new, forever home. The majority of these cats are loyal, devoted, well-trained pets who just got the short end of the bone for one reason or another and have no place to go.

If you are ready to take the leap and adopt a Siamese, then you need to do some prep work before you stroll into your local shelter. You will need to ensure that your new pet will mesh with your lifestyle and family.

Although you may want to adopt your Siamese from a rescue, it can be difficult to know where to begin. Start by phoning local veterinarian clinics to ask for recommendations. They often know of Siamese cats who might need re-homing or of reputable shelters in the area that might have a Siamese cat up for adoption. Another option is to do a Google search online for shelters or rescues in your country or state.

Sadly, some rescue shelters are just out to make money and lie to adopters, leaving them with aggressive, sick, pregnant, or even dying cats. Adopting your Siamese cat from an unethical shelter can quickly turn into a nightmare for you and your family.

THE MAJORITY OF SHELTERS ARE HONEST AND GREAT TO WORK WITH, BUT HERE ARE SOME WARNING SIGNS TO WATCH FOR WHEN ADOPTING:

- The shelter refuses to let you meet your Siamese cat before adoption day. Most reputable shelters will let you meet with your cat as often as you like, even if you are still thinking it over. Just remember, though, someone else might adopt your Siamese cat while you are in the "thinking it over" stage.
- The shelter refuses to take the adopted cat back. The majority of reputable shelters have a clause in the contract to allow you to return the cat within a specified time frame if something goes wrong. Hopefully, your Siamese cat will never have to return to the shelter.
- The shelter adopts out Siamese kittens younger than eight weeks. By law, a shelter has to vaccinate and neuter/spay animals before putting them up for adoption. Also, it is unethical and illegal to spay or neuter a kitten younger than sixteen weeks in many states.

- The shelter provides no or little proof of vaccinations. Avoid any shelter that is unwilling to provide proof of vaccinations.
- The shelter staff reminds you of pushy used-car salesmen. A good shelter is more concerned about the cat's long-term care than making a sale. They will give you the time you need with the feline to make your decision without pressure.

Many shelters provide free pamphlets or information sheets regarding the adoption process, requirements, and information on how to care for your Siamese cat. Each shelter or rescue organization has different requirements before starting the adoption process.

Photo Courtesy of Tiziana Lulja

THE FOLLOWING IS A GENERAL GUIDELINE. THE REQUIREMENTS MIGHT VARY FROM EACH SHELTER:

- Most shelters will require you to show a government-issued photo ID, proving you are twenty-one years or older.
- You will need to fill out an application form and/or an in-depth questionnaire.
- In some cases, you will need to provide references, such as permission from your landlord, verifying you are allowed to have pets.
- Some shelters or rescues will send a representative to your home to make sure it is safe and suitable for a cat.
- The shelter will observe how you and your family interact with the cat during a meet and greet before taking him home.
- Adoption fees will vary depending on the institution. Generally, the fee covers basic veterinary care, food, housing, and care the cat received while in the shelter or foster care.
- Some shelters request to follow the new pet owner's social media accounts to ensure the adopted cat is being well taken care of.

Tips for Adoption

Once you start meeting different Siamese cats who are available for adoption, your emotions will be running high. For this reason, it is important that you do your research in advance. Be sure to read the adoption contract completely before signing and always ask the following questions:

1. Is the shelter responsible for any immediate health issues? Some shelters provide two-week health coverage in case health conditions unexpectedly pop up, while other shelters expect the adopter to assume complete responsibility from day one.

2. Is your Siamese neutered or spayed? Many shelters automatically neuter or spay any cats in their charge, but others will charge extra for the surgery.

3. Can the shelter provide you with copies of your cat's medical records or background information?

4. What is the shelter's return policy? Many shelters have rules in case the adoption doesn't work out. Many shelters require the adopters to return the cat to them, even if it is years later.

If you are still on the fence about whether you should adopt your Siamese, here are a few common myths about adopting a Siamese cat:

I don't know what I'm getting – Often, when shelter cats are fostered, their foster parents will gladly share with you a wealth of information about your Siamese cat. Some shelters will also be able to tell you in detail about the Siamese's personality traits, behavior, and history.

HELPFUL TIP
Make a House Call

Making sure that your Siamese breeder is trustworthy can be a daunting prospect. Visiting your breeder's cattery or home is one way to ensure your breeder is doing things right. Some breeders will not allow kitten visitation until the kittens have been vaccinated, but you should be able to view the other cats in the home. The cattery should be clean, and the cats should look well taken care of.

I cannot find a shelter that has Siamese – Since Siamese cats are a pedigree breed, it can be hard to locate a shelter with a cat that fits your criteria. That said, many shelters maintain a waiting list for specific breeds, so don't be shy about asking to be included on their list. Other excellent options are *Petfinder.com* and *adopt-a-pet.com*, as they will help you find a Siamese cat in your locality that is up for adoption. Simply enter your zip code and the type of cat you are seeking.

Shelter cats have emotional baggage – Rescued cats have a history, but their past may be a blessing in disguise as they will already be potty-trained and have a basic understanding of obedience training. All cats, no matter their age, whether kittens or seniors, have a distinct personality. The shelter staff will help you find the ideal Siamese whose personality fits with your lifestyle.

Shelter cats were abandoned because they all have behavior issues – Quite often, cats are given up because of an unexpected change of circumstances, such as divorce, allergies, moving into housing that doesn't allow pets, financial issues, or lack of time.

Finding a Reputable Siamese Cat Breeder

Purchasing a Siamese kitten is a huge commitment, and finding a reputable breeder will not only connect you with your perfect kitty, but you can rely on them throughout your cat's life. Breeders are often likened to having your own private guide, as they will provide invaluable information, from choosing the right kitten for you to how to care for it year after year.

When choosing a Siamese cat, avoid pet stores or online websites, as the majority of these kittens come from kitten mills. A kitten mill is an inhumane, mass-breeding facility for purebred cats. These cats receive little to no human interaction, often go without medical attention, and live in their own waste.

Kitten mills are only concerned with churning out kittens for profit and completely ignore the needs of kittens and their mothers. Often, kitten mills sell through social media, online classified advertisements, flea markets, and pet stores.

Mother cats will spend their entire life in a cramped cage with little personal attention, and when they are unfit to breed, they are dumped on the side of the road or killed. Due to a lack of sanitation and medical care, the majority of kittens suffer from health issues and are prone to hereditary conditions like respiratory disorders and heart diseases.

No one knows for sure how many kitten mills there are in the United States, as they are more easily hidden from view than puppy mills. The sad truth is the only way kitten and puppy mills will ever disappear is if people stop purchasing pets on impulse through pet shops and online.

HERE ARE SOME CLUES THAT INDICATE THE BREEDER IS RUNNING A KITTEN MILL:

- The so-called breeder offers more than one type of pedigree breed.
- The breeder sells kittens less than eleven weeks or younger.
- The cattery is located in another state but is willing to ship the kitten without a face-to-face meeting with you.
- The breeder has no Grand Champions in the breeding stock. He or she breeds only pets and is not interested in improving the breed or the genetic health of the breed.
- The breeder does not ask any questions, and you can pay for the kitten up front without a screening.
- The breeder makes no future commitment to you or the cat. Reputable breeders always require you to sign a contract, promising you will return the cat to them if you are unable to care for it in the future.
- The breeder is often desperate to sell the kittens, often lowering the price when they see that you are losing interest. Good breeders do not worry whether someone will take their cats or not, as they choose their kittens' future owners based on what is best for the cat, not based on profit.

As with everything in life, it is important to do your research before signing a contract with the breeder. The best way to find a reputable Siamese breeder is by asking for a referral from a local veterinarian, friends, or at a local cat show.

HERE ARE A FEW HELPFUL SUGGESTIONS TO HELP YOU FIND A REPUTABLE SIAMESE BREEDER:

Visit the breeder at home – The best way to get to know a breeder is by visiting their home. If it is not possible to meet face to face, then organize a video-conferencing call to meet the breeder and the Siamese cats. During the meet-and-greet session, observe the breeder and cats. Does the breeder seem genuinely concerned about the well-being of the cats? Are the cats clean and well-fed? How do the cats interact with the breeder and strangers?

Any reputable breeder knows that a future owner must see the kittens in their home environment. They will be proud to show off the high-quality care they give to their cats. However, an untrustworthy breeder will have excuses as to why you cannot visit their home. They might say the litter was recently vaccinated, or there is no need to disturb the kittens.

Meet the Siamese kitten's parents – The best way to get a glimpse into how your kitten will be as an adult is to observe her parents. This will give you an excellent sense of your Siamese's personality traits, behavior, size, and appearance. When you meet the kitten and her mother, check for any abnormalities on the head, eyes, ears, nose, coat, and tummy. If the cats have treatable infections, such as mites or fleas, it is a clear indication the breeder is not responsible.

Photo Courtesy of Cindy-Leigh Thorne

Ask to see a FULL medical history – Any reputable breeder will gladly show your Siamese kitten's parents' clean bill of health and proof of health screenings. Typically, a reputable breeder will inform you about any potential health conditions that affect Siamese cats and how to prevent them.

Be patient – A reputable breeder often will have one or two litters a year, meaning you might have to wait a few months before you can welcome your little kitten home. Normally, the breeder will not let you take your Siamese home until after three months, so it can mature and learn to socialize with its littermates.

Be prepared to be interviewed – Most reputable breeders will require any potential kitten owners to fill out an extensive application form to allow them to see if you are a good fit for one of their kittens. This helps them ensure their kittens go to loving, forever homes. Some breeders have started requesting to follow the new pet owner's social media accounts to ensure their pets are going to safe, loving homes.

Ask questions – When you meet with the breeder for the first time, be prepared with a list of questions about your Siamese. Reputable breeders will happily answer all of your questions, as they want to see their kittens go to good, loving owners.

No Shipping – A reputable breeder will absolutely refuse to ship you one of their cats via plane, bus, or train. Cats and kittens can easily be stressed while traveling, causing them to get sick. For this reason, any trustworthy breeder will require you to come pick up your cat personally at their cattery, or they will deliver the cat to you for an additional fee.

Important Questions to Ask the Breeder

Before you can bring your Siamese kitten home, you will need to do some casual detective work to assess the breeder. Buying a Siamese cat is a big investment and commitment, so logically you want to make sure to get a healthy and happy Siamese from a breeder you can trust.

The list below is intended to provide you with a starting point for questions you should ask a reputable Siamese cat breeder.

Why do you breed Siamese cats?

The majority of Siamese breeders are extremely passionate about their cats and can talk for hours about how wonderful their cats and kittens are. If you contact a breeder who seems unenthusiastic, lacks passion, or seems unsure about the breed's characteristics, then it is probably best to look elsewhere.

Do you have any references?

Ask the breeder to send you a list of references. Call their clients and ask their opinions on the breeder, if they are happy with their Siamese kittens, etc.

Can I see the parents' health certification?

Generally speaking, Siamese cats are very healthy. Most health issues are hereditary, and a reputable breeder will be able to share past health certificates from the cats' family history. Any reputable breeder will include a clause in the contract guaranteeing the kitten is completely free from hereditary illnesses, often promising to return your money or give you another Siamese kitten within an established time period if the kitten you purchase falls ill.

Which registering body are the parents and kittens registered with?

In the USA, all pedigree cats must be registered with either The International Cat Association (TICA), Cat Fanciers' Association (AKC), or World Cat Congress (WCF). Siamese cats that have been used for breeding or studs must have a specialized registration to ensure the kitten litter can be registered. Never purchase an unregistered pedigree Siamese kitten, as you will not have a leg to stand on if something goes wrong, and you will not be able to professionally show or breed your cat. But please also note that registration alone is not proof enough that a breeder is reputable.

Can I visit your cattery?

Any reputable breeder will happily allow you to visit their facilities, but keep in mind that they are often very busy, so you may have to arrange an appointment ahead of time. When you visit, the facilities should be clean, tidy, and indoors. Never purchase a kitten who is raised in the garage, shed, or a cage outdoors. The cats should look in good health.

Can I meet the parents?

It might not always be possible to meet the father cat, but it is essential to see how the kitten interacts with its mother and littermates. Is the mother aggressive, shy, or well-adjusted? Are the kittens hyperactive or docile? Observe the size of the parents and their temperament. This will give you a general idea of what your cat will be like. Ask to see any other cats that may also share the home.

How do you socialize the kittens?

Kittens learn proper social skills from their mother and littermates. Ideally, the breeder is raising the kitties in a family environment, where they are exposed to adults, children, and a variety of noises. Most reputable breeders will begin potty training the kittens as soon as they begin to wander. If you have special requirements, such as socializing with a dog, it would be wise to try to find a breeder who raises their cats with dogs.

How old does the kitten have to be to come home with me?

Unlike non-pedigree cats, Siamese cats must be fully vaccinated before leaving the breeder's premises. The final vaccination should be administered no earlier than eleven to twelve weeks of age. The breeder will keep the kitten a week after the vaccination to ensure there are no adverse reactions to the vaccine. A reputable breeder will never permit their kittens to be purchased before twelve to thirteen weeks.

What paperwork will I receive with my kitten?

Below is a list of the minimum paperwork you should receive with your kitten:

- Insurance papers, if applicable
- Vaccination card
- Pedigree registration certificate
- Signed pedigree
- Copy of kitten agreement and receipt of payment
- Diet sheet

Most breeders will include additional items, such as general cat care items, etc. If the breeder uses a kitten agreement or contract, be sure to check the content before you agree to buy the kitten.

Do you professionally show your cats?

Professionally showing cats is not an essential part of breeding, but often the two go hand in hand. By rule of thumb, a breeder who shows cats will know the standards for the Siamese breed and will strive to adhere to that standard to the best of their ability. However, there are many breeders who do not show their cats and still are capable of producing outstanding quality Siamese cats.

Do I have to pay a deposit?

Any reputable breeder will require a deposit to reserve a kitten in an upcoming litter. Usually, this deposit is non-refundable and ensures the future cat owner is convinced before reserving the kitten. Deposits tend to range from $150 to $300. Never pay a deposit on a kitten who has not been born yet, as no breeder can guarantee what they will get in a litter.

Breeder Contracts and Guarantees

Often, we associate signing a contract with buying a house or leasing a car, not bringing home a little kitten!

Even though the idea of signing a contract can sound intimidating, for many breeders, it is an opportunity to share their philosophies, advice, and expectations with the new pet owner. Breeders are taking a leap of faith to entrust their defenseless, beloved kittens to a stranger. By signing a contract, you are reminded of the enormous responsibility you are about to undertake.

Although contracts can vary slightly, here are some of the basic elements you can expect to see:

- If the buyer is unable to care for the Siamese cat, then the family will return the cat to the breeder.
- If the cat is being used as a stud or for breeding, then the contract will specify the terms. Often a Siamese cat used for breeding will have a considerably higher price.
- If the cat is not planned for breeding, then the contract will specify when the cat will have to be spayed or neutered.
- The buyer must follow the specified schedule of vaccinations. Some contracts are very specific as to what type of vaccinations should be administered and when.
- The kitten is to be isolated for a week from all other household pets to minimize stress and to bond with you.

If there is anything in the contract you have difficulty understanding or are unsure about, do not sign. Make sure you completely understand what you are signing beforehand. You can ask the breeder to send you a copy of the contract in advance, so you can read it carefully without feeling pressured.

HEALTH GUARANTEES AND CERTIFICATES

Siamese cats are low maintenance when it comes to their health. But a kitten's long-term health will be directly affected by the health of her parents. For this reason, reputable breeders will go above and beyond to ensure you will receive a healthy cat who will live out a full and healthy life by your side.

Any reputable breeder will be able to share with you copies of your Siamese cat's lineage, proving past parents and grandparents have all been tested for Progressive Retinal Atrophy (PRA).

Unfortunately, Siamese cats are prone to some genetic forms of cancer. A reputable breeder will gladly share the health history of their cats to prove there is no history of cancer in their lines.

The contract should state the Siamese kitten has been vet checked and is parasite, ringworm, flea and ear mite free, as well as Feline HIV (FIV) and Feline Leukemia (FeLV) free. If the contact does not state the above, then do not trust this breeder.

Most reputable breeders will go above and beyond by taking extra precautions, testing their cats' DNA for one or all of the following: Campylobacter coli, Campylobacter jejuni, Clostridium difficile toxins A/B, feline parvovirus (feline panleukopenia), Giardia spp, Salmonella, and Tritrichomonas foetus.

Male vs. Female

One cannot help but wonder if one sex is better than the other when it comes to choosing a new feline friend to join your family. Some people affirm male cats are more affectionate while female cats are more independent.

According to veterinarians and cat breeders, when it comes to cats, there is no superior sex, and choosing a cat based on its sex will not guarantee you will get a cuddly kitten or an independent one. The environment a cat is raised in and the personality of the pet parent can often influence behavior more than genetics will.

The sex of your future kitten should not have a major bearing on your decision. Instead, you should make sure that the cat's personality and energy level is a match for yours.

It is worth mentioning that many of the biological differences between female and male cats are related to their reproductive hormones. Once the cat is neutered or spayed, the hormonal behavior will disappear over time.

Even though both male and female cats are excellent choices, there are a few physical, hormonal, and behavior differences that you should be aware of:

Physical differences – Male cats tend to be slightly larger when compared to their female littermates. Female cats tend to mature faster than male cats, making them easier to train.

Hormonal differences – Unneutered male cats have a tendency to roam in search of a mate and to mark their territory by peeing on everything. Also, they will have an innate urge to mount anything that moves, even inanimate objects. Female cats that have not been spayed will experience estrus (heat cycle) twice a year, producing a secretion to attract male cats.

Behavioral differences – There are not many behavioral differences between female and male cats. Your Siamese cat's behavior will be directly influenced by his training, upbringing, and surroundings. However, studies show that cats tend to get along better with the opposite sex. If you are bringing a second cat into your home, create the perfect balance with a female or male kitten.

Although there are some behavioral differences between male and female cats as they develop from kittens to cats, the cat's environment plays the main role in how well the two of you will bond. Instead of focusing on the sex of the Siamese cat, choose a kitten whose personality, behavior, and demeanor will meld with your lifestyle.

One Cat or More?

> *Siamese do very well being solitary cats, but they often do better as pairs. They are intelligent, curious, and active. Having a companion will keep them happier and much more active, especially if their human family is busy. Having a pair does not mean they will not give their humans attention! Oh, no. Siamese are abundant in their attention and love; they will still devote themselves to their people.*
>
> KAREN SPOHN
> *Candi Dasa cattery*

Will your Siamese cat need a feline companion? It really depends on you and your lifestyle. Siamese cats do not do well if they are left alone for long periods of time. If you will not be home for extended periods of time, then your Siamese cat will definitely be happier with another cat around.

One of the special characteristics that make Siamese cats a unique breed is their desire for social interaction. This breed loves to play and snuggle with their owners, but often owners don't have the energy to constantly entertain their cats. For this reason, many Siamese cat owners choose to remedy this problem by owning two cats.

As mentioned before, Siamese cats are very intelligent, often too bright for their own good. If they do not have something to keep them entertained and occupied, they will usually end up getting into trouble. The expression "curiosity killed the cat" can easily be applied to a Siamese cat who is left alone for too long of a period.

UNSUITABLE COMPANIONS FOR YOUR SIAMESE CAT

Even though Siamese cats are extremely sociable, not every pet would make an ideal companion. Here are a few cats to watch out for when considering adding a Siamese kitten into the family.

- **Older cats** – Siamese cats need a companion who can match their high energy. Older cats often have little desire to play with a rambunctious kitten.
- **Independent cats** – Some cats have a laid-back personality and prefer a peaceful environment; these types of cats do not make good playmates for a hyperactive Siamese cat. Some laid-back breeds are the independent Persian and short-haired British shorthair cats.

Siamese kittens need a companion who can match their spunk and affection. This breed is ideal for a family with children and other pets and for people who can give these cats the love and attention they deserve.

How to Choose a Siamese Kitten

> *When picking out a Siamese to add to the family either from a breeder or a rescue, it is always best to find the one that clicks with you. If you can pick up the cat and hold it like a baby or are able to hold the cat/kitten without it trying to bite or scratch you, then that is the cat you want. You do not want a scared, angry, or irritated cat to add to your home. You always want to make sure the kitten is at least 12 weeks old. Why do I say this? Well, because kittens that stay with their mom and littermates until at least 12 weeks develop better social skills when introducing them to their new homes and new fur siblings. This also helps with hygiene. Taking a kitten away too soon can create some habits that can be difficult to correct.*
>
> AMANDA WILLIAMS
> *AW Cattery*

Some Siamese cat breeders will have a waiting list for each expected litter, and kittens are chosen according to who is first on the list. But often, the breeder will recommend a certain kitten for the future pet owner taking into consideration their life-style and the kitten's personality to ensure an ideal mesh.

One of the best methods for choosing your Siamese kitten is observing the kitten interact with its mother and littermates, as it will give you a quick glimpse into the feline temperament and personality.

Siamese cats that are raised in a family environment are more socially adjusted to the typical household commotion. The kitten should feel comfortable around strangers and not shy away from you. If the kitten seems anxious around the breeder or you, she most likely will grow up to be a nervous cat.

Avoid choosing the bold, pushy kitten, as he may grow up to be an aggressive cat who is difficult to train. Instead, befriend the quieter kitty who already has excellent manners. However, avoid kittens that tuck their tails under their legs or pull away from you when you try to pat them. Shy cats often grow up into adult cats who are easily frightened and may snarl and scratch younger children.

Watch how each kitten interacts with her littermates and how she acts when she is apart from them. Assessing the Siamese cat's reaction will give you a general idea of how she will act in your house when she is temporarily left alone.

Give the little kitten a quick health check by making sure she is in tip-top shape. Your Siamese cat's ears should be clean and odorless. The kitten should be alert and aware of his surroundings. There should be no signs of fleas or ringworm.

If the kittens do not look healthy, then your best choice is to walk away. Even though the thought of leaving those adorable kittens behind will be difficult, it will save you from heartbreak in the future.

CHAPTER 3

Preparing for Your Siamese Cat

Welcoming a new Siamese cat or kitten into your home is an exciting experience. However, there are quite a few preparations that need to be made before bringing home your new best friend. This chapter will discuss how to plan for your new cat so that the transition as smooth as possible.

Preparations for Bringing Home a Siamese Cat

> *New cats and kittens take time to adjust to a new home. For the first three days, they may be very shy and not want to eat. Spend lots of time with the kitten, holding it, petting it, and talking. Once kittens eat in their new home, things are on the upswing. I strongly recommend starting the kitten in a safe room, which is a SMALL room like a bathroom. The food, bed, and litter box should be close. There should be minimal places for the kitten to hide. You want the kitten to interact with you, not hide. The room obviously should be safe. Check for chemicals, cleaners, electrical cords, and anything a kitten could get into that might be harmful. After a few days of bonding with you, the kitten will be ready to explore the house.*
>
> KATHLEEN RUSSELL HOOS
> *Blakewood Cattery*

Whether you are bringing home your first, second, or sixth cat, it is always important to prepare ahead of time. The following section will help you prepare for a smooth transition and integration with other family members and pets.

If you have any current pets, be sure to ensure them of your love. Before leaving to pick up the new cat, be sure to give them some cuddle time and some yummy treats. Allow them to have access to all of the areas where they were previously allowed; otherwise, they will think you are punishing them by bringing this new cat home. If you already have a cat, ensure she will have access to high areas so as to observe the new kitten from a comfortable distance.

Prepare a safe space – Create a sanctuary for the new cat that will provide the quiet and safe environment she needs while becoming familiar with her new surroundings and scents. The starter room can be any size, but it should have a secure door and a ceiling.

Photo Courtesy of Jeremy Murray

FUN FACT
Siamese Socialites

Siamese cats have a reputation for being playful and friendly, making them excellent additions to homes with other animals. In fact, Siamese cats can become lonely when their humans are away. Having another pet in the home can prevent your cat from becoming lonely. However, some dogs, particularly those with a high prey drive, may not be suited to a cat companion, so be sure to introduce your furry friends slowly and safely.

Allow the resident pets to explore the area freely before bringing home the new cat. If possible, ask the breeder to give you a piece of cloth that has the new kitten's scent. Let your current pets smell the scent, as this will help them embrace your Siamese cat quicker.

Give the cat a place to hide – Cats, in general are nervous and like to hide, even more so when they are introduced into a new environment. A cardboard box or a towel draped over a chair make ideal hiding spots for your little kitten. If you have adopted an older Siamese cat, I recommend removing larger pieces of furniture from the space, such as beds, couches, and dressers. It will be much easier to interact with a shy cat that is hiding in a box instead of one hiding under the bed.

Put food, water, and litter in the room – Place the cat's food and water dishes on one side of the room and the box of litter on the other side of the room. Adopted cats most likely will not eat much for the first twenty-four to forty-eight hours and may experience diarrhea from stress.

Give your cat a new scratching post – Place a new scratching post in the room. Scratching is a natural way for cats and kittens to destress. It is important the scratching post is new and has not been used by other cats. Your new Siamese cat does not need to be stressed by the scent of unfamiliar cats while she is adapting to her new surroundings.

In the next chapter, we will discuss how to introduce your new cat to your resident pets, such as dogs and cats.

Preparing Children and Family

Keep your Siamese cat's home-coming low-key and stress-free. Be sure to phone your friends and family ahead of time to let them know you will not be having a meet-and-greet the first day your cat comes home. The fewer new people your kitten has to meet on her first day, the better.

If you have children or grandchildren, you will need to do a few practice sessions with them before you bring home the new kitty.

Nothing excites a child more than a kitten or cat. The child will want to hug and squeeze the fluffy little cat. For this reason, it is extremely important that you sit down with your children prior to bringing home the new cat and teach them how to hold and pick up the new cat.

First impressions have never been more important, so plan ahead for a smooth transition. If the child makes a bad first impression, the kitten may be nervous around children for the rest of her life.

One of the best ways to teach younger children how to pick up and pat a kitten is by doing a few practice sessions using a stuffed toy that is the same size as the cat you will be bringing home. Explain to the child that even though your Siamese cat looks like a cuddly stuffed toy, he is not a toy, and by squeezing too hard, the child can hurt the cat. Also, tell the child that the new cat or kitten will need time to explore her new surroundings and rest.

Another detail to take into consideration is children's tendency to yell and shriek when they get excited, which will frighten the new cat. Do practice sessions with your children, helping them use softer indoor voices to avoid startling the Siamese cat.

To help introduce your new kitten to children, I've included a little message with some suggestions from cats:

Hi! I am your new cat, and I'd like to tell you a few things:

- I feel very nervous and shy because your house is brand new to me.
- Please be patient with me, as it will take me a few days to feel comfortable.
- I will play with you when I feel comfortable, so please do not chase me.
- My way of learning about my new surroundings is by smelling everything.
- I am afraid of loud voices or noises and fast movements.
- I need quiet times just like you, so I might find a warm hiding spot for a nap.
- Please pat me gently, and never pull my tail! It hurts!
- Make sure you never let me go outside; I am little like you and might get lost.
- Because I am nervous, I might hiss; that is how I say, "I am scared!"

Rule of thumb: Never leave your kitten and the child alone together, even if it is only for a minute or two. The child's and the cat's relationship need to develop under strict supervision, rewarding calm and gentle behavior.

Establish Kitten House Rules and Daily Routines

> *Don't put breakables anywhere the cat can get them...even if you think it's high enough, it's not. Have lots of lightweight, soft toys on hand that can be carried around. Not only do Siamese walk around with toys in their mouth, but they like to fetch and throw toys up in the air.*
>
> KATHRYN BRADY
> *Katsmith*

If you have never owned a kitten or adopted an older cat, you will need to prepare yourself and your family for cat ownership. Cats and kittens need love, attention, companionship, and care. But that does not mean you have to hand your house over to your new kitten. Just like human beings, kittens and cats thrive in homes where the expectations and rules are clear and easy to understand.

Have a family meeting

Before bringing your Siamese cat home, sit down with all the members of your household and agree upon a set of rules for the new kitten and each family member.

House rules only work if every single person sticks to them constantly; otherwise, your Siamese cat will be confused and not understand what is expected of her. For example, it will be impossible to teach your Siamese cat that she is not allowed on the kitchen table if your children occasionally let her hop up on the table for a treat or two.

Siamese cats are extremely intelligent and relatively easy to train, but once they get away with something, they will have a hard time accepting a firm "No" the next time. Everybody has to be on the same page when it comes to house rules — no exceptions ever! With that in mind:

- Make sure you and the rest of your family have time to spend and bond with the new cat.
- Where will your kitty spend the night? You may want to keep her in one location for the first week as it is easy to lose a little kitten who decides to hide somewhere in your big house or apartment.

- Who is responsible for kitten care? From feeding to cleaning up the litter box cleaning to vet care to grooming, cats and kittens do require a certain amount of time, work, and energy.
- Agree as a family on the rules you will establish for the new cat. May she sleep on the furniture? What is the rule about jumping up on the kitchen countertops or onto the table?
- Will you feed the kitten table scraps? Siamese cats have a healthy appetite. If you give your cat a treat under the table occasionally, then she will learn to beg for more food. Begging is one of the hardest bad habits to break, so it is best to avoid it completely.

Establishing a routine and house rules are essential for your Siamese cat. Your kitten will be eager to adapt to her new family and understand what is expected of her. The more consistent the entire household is at following rules, the sooner your kitty will figure everything out.

You have just taken the defenseless kitten from the only world she has ever known, leaving her mother and littermates behind. Your kitty has just had a terrifying car ride and has arrived in a strange world with new scents, sounds, and people. Your Siamese cat needs to learn how to live and adapt to her new environment. By establishing your new cat's rules ahead of time, you will help her grow into a well-behaved and well-mannered member of your family in no time.

Kitten Proofing Your Home

Having a sturdy house is a must! Things that are easily knocked over or things that are breakable should be put up or put in a display case. Pictures on shelves should be Velcro-d in place. This helps keep the pictures in place if the kitty wants to climb and explore. Keeping cabinets that have cleaning supplies locked or child-proofed is always good to do. Getting cat runs to put up around your house is always a must. This will help your cat burn off extra energy!

AMANDA WILLIAMS
AW Cattery

Siamese cats, especially kittens, are like toddlers and can get themselves into trouble very fast. All cats are curious little tykes and love to explore nooks and crannies. Whether you are about to be a new kitten owner or a veteran, you will need to kitten proof your entire home. There will be no need to kitten proof outside of your house, as Siamese cats are indoor cats.

Photo Courtesy of Christina Leaf

Ever heard of the old expression "curiosity killed the cat?" That expression could not be truer when it comes to a Siamese cat as their great sense of smell can quickly get them into trouble. You will need to take precautions to protect your Siamese kitten and your house from potential disaster. For example:

- Cats, but even more so kittens, are fascinated by anything that moves and by anything that they can move around with their paws. This includes knick-knacks, straw baskets, wires, bathroom items, and tablecloths. Some of these items can be a danger for your little kitten or disastrous for fragile decorations or dinner.
- Your Siamese cat has long legs, and they will climb almost anything they can. Beware! Your kitten will slip through unlatched windows or open doors if left unattended.
- Siamese cats adore sharpening their claws and often cannot tell the difference between their scratching post and your carpet or sofa.
- Cats and kittens have their nose close to the ground, which means their great sense of smell will be able to sniff out the tiniest piece of rubbish on the floor.
- Kittens do not have the ability to tell the difference between their food and safe treats and potentially harmful human food. In Chapter Ten of this book, you can find a list of harmful foods for cats.

Before you bring home your Siamese kitten, get down on your knees and crawl from room to room, looking out for any possible hazards at a kitten's eye level. The Siamese's personality is often compared to Velcro. This means that where you are, your cat will be right by your side. For this reason, be sure to pay extra attention to rooms where you will be spending the majority of your time.

IN THE KITCHEN

Food and the alluring scent of garbage are the most attractive elements of your kitchen for your curious Siamese cat. Siamese cats love to seek out scents with their noses, so never under estimate your kitty being left alone in the kitchen. While your Siamese is still a kitten, you may want to place her in a kitten playpen inside of your kitchen.

Your cabinets and drawers are ideal cubby holes to crawl into and explore. You can buy childproof latches at the local hardware store, which will help to prevent your curious kitty from getting into trouble, and at the same time, keep her away from harmful cleaning supplies and foods. In

Chapter Ten, you will find an extensive list of human foods that are considered toxic for all cats.

Your Siamese cat's nose can sniff out the tiniest morsel of food on the floor, and your garbage bin will be almost impossible to resist. If you do not want to find your floors littered with garbage, then make sure your garbage bin has a tight lid that tightly closes, or better yet, keep it tucked away under the sink with a childproof lock on the door.

IN THE LIVING AREAS

Look around your living areas, at high shelves, ow cupboards, and hidden nooks. Could your kitten jump onto a shelf holding valuables or fragile items? Could your kitty become trapped inside of a cupboard? Fold and secure all window blind cords with an elastic band and make sure all the power cords are tucked away, out of sight, or placed inside of a chew-proof PVC tube.

If you are into needlework, keep all of your supplies in a closed container. Needles and thread might seem like ideal plays toy to your kitten, but they can be fatal if your little kitty swallows them. Plastic bags and plastic wrap can also cause suffocation.

Another hazard is house plants. Many house plants are toxic if consumed by cats, such as lilies, orchids, Christmas cactus, jade plants, ivy, and

Photo Courtesy of Autumn Tucker

aloe vera. Place any house plants on a table, counter, or inside an off-limits room with the door shut. Floral arrangements may be toxic for your Siamese cat, so check before putting them in a location your cat can reach.

If you have a fireplace, your Siamese cat will be instantly attracted to it as they love heat, but she can be easily harmed by ashes and flames. A quick and easy solution is to use a protective fire screen.

IN THE OFFICE

Your office is full of everyday items that will make your Siamese cat feel like she is inside of a candy shop with endless temptations, such as paper clips, staples, rubber bands, and so on. It might be entertaining to watch your cat play with these items, but if accidentally swallowed, they can cause a serious problem, even being fatal on some occasions.

Wires and computer cords resemble a snake, making them almost irresistible to your curious little kitten. Be sure to keep them stapled to a wall or covered with a PVC tube. Cloth drapes are better left out of reach of your furry curtain climber. Tie them up securely until your Siamese cat is taught to use a scratching post.

IN THE BATHROOM

Keep your toilet seat lid down at all times, or your cat may fall in or drink from it. Furthermore, sinks and tubs filled with water may present a drowning hazard for your kitty. Keep your bathroom off-limits to your kitten unless you absolutely have to keep her litter box in there.

Some hazards in the bathroom are quite obvious, such as dental floss, medications, razors, cotton swabs, or soap. These can all be dangerous if eaten or swallowed by your kitty. Expensive emergency visits to the veterinarian's office are quite common for kittens. Be sure to place all shampoos, conditioners, tissue paper, etc., inside of the bathroom cabinet or on a shelf out of the cat's reach.

IN THE BEDROOM

Remember, your Siamese kitten is scent-oriented and will gravitate towards anything that smells like you, such as your leather shoes or your exercise shorts. Bedrooms are generally benign when it comes to kitten hazards. But to be on the safe side, make sure any jewelry, hair clips, hairpins, and bands are out of your curious cat's reach.

Mothballs are another potential hazard. They are extremely toxic, so if you use them, make sure they are stored in a place your Siamese cat cannot reach. Dirty, smelly clothes are especially tempting for your Siamese kitten, so be sure to place them inside a laundry hamper.

IN THE GARAGE OR THE BASEMENT

Do not let your kitten into the garage or basement unsupervised, and always keep the doors closed. Garages and basements tend to be storage areas for just about everything, including pesticides, rodent poison, fertilizers, antifreeze, solvents, coolants, gasoline, and so on. Antifreeze is very tasty to cats and is one of the most poisonous substances for animals. If you live in a colder climate, be aware that many de-icing compounds are made from harmful chemicals, so look for a product that is pet safe.

IN THE LAUNDRY

Always keep the door to your clothes dryer closed, and double-check inside before using it. All cats, including kittens, like to find dark, warm places to sleep, and the results could be tragic. Make sure laundry detergents, bleach, and fabric softeners are up off the floor and inside of a closed cabinet.

IN THE YARD

If you decide to take your Siamese cat outside either on a leash or inside of a playpen, you will need to take certain precautions. Compost, mulches, pesticides, insecticides, fertilizers, and other garden chemicals can cause health issues for your kitty. Your best line of defense is to use products on your lawn and garden that are pet-friendly.

There are a number of indoor and outdoor plants that can cause gastrointestinal issues such as diarrhea and vomiting. Some of the most common outdoor plants that are toxic for cats are daffodils, foxglove, tulips, bird of paradise, and lupines. Be sure to block off access to your plants anytime your kitten is roaming the yard under your supervision. You can find a more extensive list of toxic plants for cats on the Animal Poison Control website.

BETTER SAFE THAN SORRY

As mentioned before, kittens are similar to toddlers. Imagine a toddler wandering into your home, touching anything that looks interesting and putting it into their mouth or shredding it to pieces. Next, imagine a little kid who can climb, leap, and zip past you without making a sound, and you have a good idea why you need to take precautions.

As a general precaution, be sure to put away anything of value or that could be a choking hazard (bobby-pins, puzzle pieces, Air-pods, etc.) when you are not around.

Open doors and windows are great at letting in fresh air, but they can also tempt your Siamese cat outside into the world of cars and other risks. If you like to open the windows or doors, make sure they are properly sealed with a screen to prevent your curious cat from escaping.

Christmas time presents a long list of hazards for your little kitten. Avoid dampening your holiday cheer with emergency veterinary visits by following these tips:

- Barricade your Christmas tree behind a baby gate or pen to keep your cat out. Ornaments and lights look like excellent batting and chewing toys to your cat.
- Double-check your tree placement, as Siamese cats can jump high and can accidentally knock the tree over. Consider keeping your tree in a people-only room, if possible.
- Beware of poisonous holiday plants, such as mistletoe, holly, lilies, and amaryllis.

By taking the time now to kitten-proof your home, you are setting your cat up for success. As your Siamese gets older, she will learn the house rules and understand what is expected of her, so there will not be a need to be so vigilant.

Shopping List

Once you bring your new Siamese cat home, whether she's an adult or a kitten, you will not want to leave your furry bundle of joy alone while you go shopping, so make sure you get the following items beforehand. In the excitement of bringing your kitten home, you do not want to suddenly discover just before bedtime that you forgot to buy cat food.

The most indispensable item on the list? Your unconditional love — it may sound cheesy, but it is true.

Appropriate food - Often, the shelter or breeder will give you a few days' worth of the food they were already feeding the cat. If you acquire your kitten from a breeder, more often than not, their contract will specify you feed the kitten a certain type of food for at least the first few months.

Food and water bowls – Even though your cat can use any ceramic (non-lead-glazed) or stainless-steel bowls you have in your kitchen, you may feel more comfortable providing her with her own dishes. It is not recommended to use plastic dishes for cats as some Siamese cats can develop a chin rash from plastic, and softer plastic easily scratches, providing places for bacteria growth. To be on the safe side, purchase only products made in the U.S.

Automatic water dispensers – All cats love the taste of fresh, running water, and automatic dispensers ensure a constant supply of clean water.

Cat carrier – This is a necessity! Never try to transport your cat without one. The breeder or shelter may supply you with a simple cardboard box one for the first journey home, but after that, you will need to replace it with

Photo Courtesy of Tom Jimmerson

a solid-bottomed fiberglass or sturdy plastic carrier. The carrier should provide enough room for your Siamese cat to stand up, turn around, and stretch.

Scratching post – A scratching post is an absolute must as your cat is going to scratch, whether you approve or not. There are endless models and styles with varying price tags. Some scratching posts have added a catnip scent to attract your kitty.

Grooming tools – Even if you plan to get your Siamese cat professionally groomed, you should have all the basics at home. Pet-friendly shampoo, a comb, a brush, and nail clippers are essential grooming tools. You can find more information on how to groom your kitty in Chapter Eleven of this book.

Kitty treats – Kitty treats play a vital role in training your four-pawed companion. Look for treats that are soft, chewable, and low in calories and sugar. Remember that while treats help in bonding and reinforcing good behavior, they should never make up more than 10% of your cat's overall diet.

Litter box and litter – Choosing the best litter box for your Siamese cat is essential for your indoor cat. If you adopted an older cat, look for a sizeable box with high sides, as they tend to throw the litter around a bit. Kittens will need a box with lower sides to allow them to easily enter and leave.

There are various types of litter. Avoid clumping clay litter as it contains a toxic ingredient that is harmful if ingested by your cat. All clay litter tends to stir up dust that is not healthy to breathe, either for you or your cat.

It is helpful to place a mat under the box to catch any stray litter. You can buy a litter mat at the pet store or use a carpet or linoleum sample that you can toss when it gets too grungy.

A bed (optional but highly recommended) – Even if you plan on having your cat sleep with you on your bed, it is still a good idea to provide your kitten with her own special, cozy place for napping. Make sure the bed is soft, comfortable, washable, and big enough for an adult cat to curl up comfortably but not so big that she feels vulnerable.

Toys – All cats need mental stimulation, including your Siamese cat, no matter how old she is. Toys are a fantastic way to bond and interact with your kitty. If your Siamese is a kitty, look for toys designed for kittens during their teething stage. Consider interactive treat toys and puzzle toys to keep your kitten engaged when you cannot be with her.

Stain and odor remover – Kittens do not come potty trained, and even if you adopted an older shelter Siamese cat, she might need to be reminded about proper indoor potty etiquette. You need to anticipate accidents. Look for a stain and odor remover that is designed to destroy pet urine enzymes.

These enzymes are like a red flag calling out for your kitten to return to the same spot to urinate again.

Cat toothpaste – You will need to get your Siamese kitten used to having her teeth brushed from the very first week of bringing her home. Good oral care is essential to your cat's overall health. Without it, bacteria can grow to develop into plaque, and plaque triggers gingivitis and eventually periodontal disease. If your cat refuses to let you brush her teeth, there are healthy water additives for her water dish with bacteria-inhibiting enzymes.

Collar, leash, and harness (optional) – It is highly recommended that your Siamese cat wear a collar with ID tags. It may take some time to get her used to wearing the collar before putting on the ID tags. If you plan on teaching your cat to walk on a leash, get her used to her harness and leash by using it inside of the house.

Make a vet appointment – This might not be an item for your shopping list, but unless your Siamese cat comes with proof of a recent veterinary visit, proof of vaccinations, a negative test for several diseases and medical conditions, then your first stop before bringing her home is the veterinary clinic. Make the appointment a few weeks in advance before picking up your kitten.

Choosing a Vet

Finding a trustworthy veterinarian is a decision that should not be taken lightly.

If you are a new cat owner, you will need to find a veterinarian for your new Siamese cat before you bring home her home. This section will help you choose the perfect vet. Choosing the right vet for your Siamese cat is something you will need to consider carefully, as they will be your cat's main healthcare practitioner.

Word of mouth

Asking friends and family is one of the best ways to find a reputable veterinarian in your locality. Be sure to ask fellow cat lovers in your area for advice on different options in your area. If your Siamese cat's breeder is from your locality, they will happily recommend their veterinarian.

Find a veterinarian with expertise treating felines

Not all veterinarians are created equal. Some veterinarians specialize in certain types of animals, such as cows, horses, pigs, and other non-feline pets. You definitely want a veterinarian whose expertise is in treating and caring for cats. Be sure to ask the vet how much experience he has treating cats like your Siamese.

Consider the cost and location

In the unlikely event an emergency occurs, will you be able to get to the vet's clinic quickly? Be sure to choose a veterinarian whose clinic is less than a one-hour drive from your house, and ask if they make house calls to your area. Costs vary from vet to vet, so do not forget to inquire about their prices and choose a clinic whose prices fit your budget.

Look for a clean facility

Ask to have a look around the office to check the level of cleanliness. If the place seems dirty, dingy, or foul-smelling, then that is a sign to move on. A veterinarian's office is a medical facility, so it should be just as clean as a hospital or clinic for humans.

Look for licensed personnel

Most of us just assume that all veterinarians are licensed professionals, but that is not always the case. Make sure the vet is licensed in your state as a veterinarian and not just as a registered veterinary technician. On the American Animal Hospital Association (AAHA) website, you will find a list of accredited and licensed veterinarians in your locality, as well as an evaluation of the facility, staff, patient care, and equipment.

Inquire about their approach to medicine and cats

Most vets have different approaches when it comes to pets and medication. Be sure to have a brief discussion with the potential vet to see if his philosophies about wellness and prevention match with yours. If they are not on the same page as you, then you should move on.

Personal referrals are a great start, but you should still take time to research the veterinary clinic and its staff. The vet you finally choose will play a significant role in your Siamese cat's life, so take your time looking for the right one.

By being prepared for your new Siamese cat's arrival, you will be able to concentrate on bonding with her as soon as you bring her home. Besides making your Siamese cat feel like a member of the family, do not forget to capture your memories together through your camera or phone.

CHAPTER 4

What to Expect the First Few Weeks

> *Siamese are very different from most tabby cats. They are much more sensitive to social change and are a bit lost when moving into their new homes. I tell new owners to start their new kittens in a small space, such as a half bath. Come home and sit in the room with your kitten for 20 minutes, speaking to and comforting your kitten. Then leave the kitten alone for 20 minutes with a warm spot, litter box, clean water, and a couple of pieces of dry food. Return after that 20-minute absence, offer a small taste of food, and again, comfort and play with the kitten. This process should continue until the kitten is missing you rather than being fearful. This usually doesn't take more than a few visits. I like my kittens to be picked up early in the day so that they are acclimated by bed-time and can hopefully snuggle in a bed. Once a kitten is looking for its new owner rather than being fearful, you can expand the space the kitten has access to.*
>
> CAROLE PULKOWSKI
> *Abha Siamese*

You are about to embark on the fun and occasionally crazy world of Siamese cat parenthood. For the next twelve to seventeen years, you are going to receive more love and affection than you will know what to do with. This chapter will prepare you for the first few days with your Siamese cat so that you and your furry friend can have a great start to your new life together!

The Ride Home

The first car ride home should not be taken lightly. It is an opportunity to get off on the right paw and start bonding together. Also, there are quite a few safety aspects to take into consideration, such as how to keep you and your cat safe on the journey home. Also, how should you prepare for the ride home?

Before you head out to pick up your bundle of fur, make sure you are well-prepared by bringing along a blanket, a few chew toys, a leash and a collar, plus any cleaning supplies in case your new cat has an accident in the car.

Upon arriving at the breeder's house, any final paperwork will be dealt with outside before going inside to pick up your Siamese kitten. The breeder probably will give you a small bag of the current cat food your kitty is eating to wean her onto the new food you are planning to feed her.

To prevent car sickness, no food should be given to your kitten for two to three hours prior to traveling. If the trip home is longer than three hours, be sure to bring along her food dish to give her a small handful of food in case she gets hungry. Siamese love to eat, and when they are hungry, they will clearly let you know by meowing.

Before hopping in the car and driving off with your new Siamese cat, take her away from her mother and littermates so she can get used to being close to you. This will give your kitten an opportunity to smell you. Place your Siamese kitten in the litter box for one last chance to relieve herself before the big journey.

Let your Siamese kitten explore the car at her own pace by giving her a chance to smell her new blanket and carrying case. Make sure the doors and windows are shut and turn the car on so she won't be frightened by the engine noise.

Keeping your pet restrained in the car is highly encouraged by most veterinarians. The two main options for cat car restraints are a harness with a seat-belt attachment or a padded carrier secured by a seat belt in the back seat. It's crucial to secure your cat away from airbags, such as the back seat. Allowing your cat to roam freely in the car can be hazardous to you and your cat.

DRIVING WITH YOUR NEW CAT

It might be appealing to have your new feline friend sit beside you on the passenger seat, peering out the window, but safety should be your priority. Your kitty is not going to give you directions, but she will distract you by keeping your eyes off the road and on her, which may cause an accident. Read on to discover the best ways to travel with your new Siamese cat.

Your safety – All cats are curious by nature, and if they are not secured inside of a travel crate, they can easily and dangerously become wedged under the pedals while you are driving. Your new cat may cry or whine in the travel crate, which is a natural response.

Your Siamese cat's safety – Younger kittens lack coordination, and if allowed to wander around while the car is moving, they could possibly fall

Photo Courtesy of Annette & Joseph Keawkalaya

to the floor and hurt themselves. In addition, if you have to come to a sudden stop or swerve around a corner, your Siamese cat could be thrown off balance and be seriously injured.

Front or back seat? – In the United States, children who are seven years and younger are not permitted to sit in the front seat due to the impact of airbags. In the case of an accident, the air bag is instantly activated, releasing a punch that could seriously injure or kill a child. In the case of your itsy-bitsy Siamese kitty, the force would, without a doubt, be fatal.

Crate or carried? – Many people, understandably, just want to cuddle with their adorable little bundle of fur on the drive home. Some have a small cardboard box that they plan to place on the floor of the car, but this will not prevent a kitten from climbing over the edges and gallivanting around the car. Additionally, do not be tempted to let a passenger hold the cat because she could easily wiggle free and cause a distraction. Your best choice is to use a travel crate.

You want your Siamese to associate good memories with her crate as you will be using it for training, so take the crate out of the car and place it on the ground with a few yummy snacks inside. Let your kitten go in on her own terms so she feels safe. Place a soft blanket and chew toy inside. Crate training will be discussed later in this book.

WHEN CHOOSING A TRAVEL CARRIER, CONSIDER THE FOLLOWING POINTS:

- **Find the correct size** — A twelve-week-old Siamese kitten weighs approximately six to eight ounces and should be the size of two tennis balls. A full-grown Siamese will weigh between seven to ten pounds and range from seven to nine inches in height. The carrier or crate should be big enough for your kitten to stand up in and turn around.
- **Design matters** — Look for a cat carrier that has passed third-party crash tests and comes highly reviewed. A poorly designed cat carrier can be hazardous in an accident.
- **Choose a style** — There are two basic styles of travel carriers for cats: hard and soft cover. Hard covers offer superior protection for your cat and are preferable if traveling long distances. Soft covers offer less protection for your cat but are easier to carry.

Bathroom breaks — Take along a portable litter tray and several Ziplock baggies. Place a small amount of litter into each baggie. If possible, use a small amount of litter from the breeder so the cat will recognize the smell. If it is a long trip home, when you stop at a restroom, place the litter tray on the floor of the car and fill it with litter. You may have to wait five to ten minutes before the kitten decides to attempt going to the bathroom.

Car sickness — Many kittens and older cats suffer from car sickness. Watch for your cat pointing her nose toward the floor, lips wrinkled up, drooling and heaving. If this happens, lay a towel under her to facilitate cleanup. Cover your cat's crate with a blanket to help her feel more secure, or open the window a crack to let in fresh air.

Climatic considerations — Kittens have a difficult time regulating their body temperature and are prone to hypothermia and hyperthermia. Make sure the inside temperature of your car is comfortable, and never leave your kitty alone in the car.

Psychological well-being — Come straight home. This is not a time to stop and grab some groceries or stop off for a quick visit with friends. Keep the entire trip quick. Remember that your cat is already having an incredibly stressful day.

Two is better than one — Ask a friend or family member to go with you to pick up your Siamese kitty, as they can drive the car while you sit in the back seat next to your kitten. Siamese tend to bond quickly with people they encounter early on. Plus, remember this is the first time your cat has been for a car ride and separated from her family, so being alone can be a terrifying experience.

Make it a positive experience and avoid creating emotional scars that could resurface later on in your cat's life, such as separation anxiety. Talk to her in a soft, calming voice to make her feel safe and sound. If you play music in the car, choose something soft.

Recognizing Signs of Stress in Your Siamese

The tell-tale signs of stress often vary from cat to cat. New cat owners often notice something is not quite right with their cat after the feline has been stressed out for some time.

Stress has a debilitating effect on your cat's health, as it can aggravate existing physical conditions and cause behavioral issues, such as aggressive behavior, depression, withdrawal, and incontinence.

Cats and kittens do not like change. Even the most subtle change in a cat's environment can cause stress. Substantial changes, such as moving to a new house, can lead to considerable stress if certain precautions are not taken to alleviate your cat's stress levels.

Managing stress is an important factor for older Siamese cats or any cats with a chronic disease. Cats with Feline Immunodeficiency Virus (FIV) or Feline Leukemia Virus (FeLV) do not thrive in high-stress environments. It would be unloving to bring home a new kitten or puppy if your cat is immunocompromised.

TELL-TALE SIGNS OF STRESS

Your Siamese cat or kitten cannot explain her feelings in words, but she can show you that she is stressed out. Here are a few of the most common signs of stress in Siamese cats.

Stomach distress

Stressed cats or kittens may become physically sick when they are stressed out. They may vomit, have diarrhea, have a runny nose or watery eyes, get lethargic, or sleep more than normal. If you notice any of these symptoms persisting for more than a day, consult with your veterinarian to give your cat a clean bill of health. Then you will need to figure out what is causing your furry feline friend distress in the house.

Hiding

Hiding is one of the most obvious signs of stress or anxiety. Many cats will hide when they are not feeling well. A simple solution is to create a safe room for your Siamese cat where you can frequently check on her until the stressful situation has passed. You may need to entice your kitty to come out of her hiding place with a game or by tossing a treat or two.

Peeing outside of the litter box

Your Siamese cat is extremely intelligent and will look for different ways to communicate with you. For example, if your cat's litter box is in dire need of cleaning, she may decide to go elsewhere. Or she may decide to go in front of you, or even jump up on your bed and relieve herself to let you know she is not feeling well. Most kitty parents disregard this "communication" as bad behavior. An easy solution is to always keep your cat's litter box clean and remember that cats do not like to share their litter boxes with other cats.

Appetite changes

When cats are overly stressed out, they may become fussier about food choices or may completely decide not to eat. On the other hand, some cats may overeat when stressed. If your cat refuses to eat or is vocalizing that she wants to eat more food, it is a possible sign she is stressed or has a medical issue.

Cats that do not eat for a day or two can quickly get very sick. Always inform your veterinarian when your cat stops eating for a day, particularly if your cat is still a kitten or elderly. A cat who overeats is most likely suffering from boredom, so be sure to spend more time playing with your cat. Get her moving to release some of the built-up tension.

Increased vocalization

Siamese cats are already very vocal, but when they are upset about something, they begin to vocalize more. You will notice your cat will try to show you what is upsetting her, as she will often look at something while vocalizing, such as a dirty litter box, a bed that was moved to a new spot, or an empty food dish.

There are several different situations that might cause your cat anxiety and stress. Cats, especially Siamese cats, are creatures of habit, so any sudden change in their day-to-day routine can be a trigger for stress.

Veterinary visits

The majority of cats tend to be frightened going to the veterinarian, with so many strange scents and noises. To alleviate stress, transport your cat inside of her carrier, and place a lightweight blanket over the top until you arrive at the vet's office.

New family members (human or animal)

It is always hard to decipher how a cat will react to a new person or animal in the environment. Introducing a new roommate, baby, or spouse in the household takes time and patience. The same is true if you are bringing a new animal into the house. Let your cat come around at her own pace and avoid the urge to rush the relationship.

Moving to a new house

When moving, be sure to guarantee your cat's life is disrupted as little as possible. During the actual move, place your cat in a closed room with her favorite belongings, such as her blankie, toys, litter box, food and water, and a bed. Bring your Siamese cat and all of her belongings to the new house, and place her in a safe room as you unpack your belongings.

Be sure your cat has her own things around at all times, as she will identify as this as a piece of her home. Long-distance moves are trickier, and you may need to ask a friend to temporarily cat-sit your cat or to set up your cat's safe room ahead of time as you travel with your cat via plane, train, or car.

Change in daily routine

A sudden change in your routine, such as a new job or the kids going back to school, should be handled with care. A week or so before the change, start leaving the house at different hours and gradually increase the period of time. Upon return, be sure to praise your kitty with some playtime and attention.

Photo Courtesy of Mary E. Kvam

Loud parties and noise

Siamese cats are stressed out by holidays, as there are fireworks and the constant ringing of the doorbell from guests, accompanied by loud music, talking, and laughing. If you are planning a family get-together, take precautions by placing a "come on in" sign on the door. Choose soft background music and place your cat in her safe room with the door shut.

View through the window

Your Siamese will spend hours each day gazing out the window. However, some cats experience redirected aggression. Re-directed aggression occurs when the cat sees something outside the window, such as a raccoon, a cat-fight, or another animal strolling through the yard. The cat feels frustrated as she is unable to defend her territory and will suddenly take her aggression out on the closest human or animal. This type of stress might require that you take steps to deter the animal from exploring your yard or blocking your cat's view from the window.

HOW TO REDUCE STRESS

Once you have determined the trigger for your Siamese cat's stress, you can take measures to ease her anxiety. Often, this will require eliminating the stressor, such as by partially closing the blinds, no longer hosting loud parties, or getting a new litter box.

There are many types of natural therapies, such as homeopathic remedies or herbal essences, that may help to reduce your cat's stress and anxiety. Be sure to check with your veterinarian first before trying out any of these products, and only introduce one remedy at a time.

Pheromone sprays, diffusers, collars, and plug-ins are extremely helpful in reducing stress, as they make the cat feel more safe and secure.

In severe cases, you may need to discuss with your vet another option to help your kitty feel calmer and more relaxed. Often, in extreme cases, a veterinarian will describe an anti-anxiety medication.

One of the best methods for keeping your cat's stress down is managing your own stress levels. Take time to unwind after a stressful day at work with a cup of hot tea or a glass of wine to avoid telegraphing your stress to your cat.

The First Day

Bringing a new cat or kitten home is a joyous occasion. You have been waiting for this moment, perhaps for months. However, even though you are bursting with excitement about starting your new life with your cat, remember that she is overwhelmed and exhausted. After all, she is in a strange place, with new scents and people she doesn't know. Here is everything you need to know about making your Siamese cat's first day easier.

Your Siamese kitten is still a baby. Up until today, she had spent her entire life near her mother and littermates. All the sights, noises, and smells that once comforted her are gone and have been replaced with strange new ones. To help your kitten settle into her new home quicker, ask the breeder to give you a piece of bedding or a snuggle toy that smells like the cat's mother and littermates.

Keep your Siamese cat's homecoming low-key and stress-free. Be sure to phone your friends and family ahead of time to let them know you will not be having a meet and greet the first day your cat comes home. The fewer new people your cat has to meet on her first day, the better.

A cat from a shelter might arrive sleep-deprived or stressed, so don't be surprised if the first thing she does after exploring her surroundings is to fall into a deep slumber. Your adopted Siamese cat will need a short period of time to adjust to her new routine and structure, no matter if she was in the shelter for a few days or a couple of months. She will need to learn new habits and rules as she settles into her new forever home.

Your goal is to help your new Siamese cat get to know you and trust you. When you bring your cat home, place a piece of your clothing in the room that has your scent. There is no need to hurry and introduce your new cat to your other pets. You will have plenty of opportunities to teach them how to get along, and slower introductions will allow the animals to get acquainted with each other on their own terms.

If you have adopted an older Siamese cat who has had a traumatic past, you can use a store-bought product that imitates natural cat pheromones released by a mother cat to calm her kittens. This scent will help the older cat feel more relaxed, reduce anxiety, and help her cope better with changes.

One of the first things you need to show your Siamese cat is where her designated potty area is and her water and food dishes. This is an excellent time to start teaching your cat her new name. Within a few days, she should know it like the back of her paw. Show your new furry friend where her home

Photo Courtesy of April Tinnin Sapphire Kittens Cattery

base will be and throw some yummy snacks onto her bed so she lies down on her own accord.

Resist the urge to shower her with attention. Instead, let your Siamese cat dictate the pace of her interactions. Some cats and kittens are outgoing and enthusiastic; others might be standoffish and prefer to sit back and observe their new surroundings. Avoid chasing your Siamese cat around the house or cuddling her, even though you just want to play or snuggle her. Teach her to trust you by sitting on the ground and letting your cat come and go as she wishes.

Do not be disappointed if your kitten hides. Hiding is a coping mechanism, so do not disturb her. Once your kitty feels confident and comfortable, she will venture out on her own accord. Avoid the urge to hunch down and stare at your new cat, as direct staring is aggressive body language to a cat, so if you want to admire your new cat, be sure to do so from the corner of your eye.

Be sure to spend time with your new Siamese cat in her safe space. On the day you plan to bring your feline friend home, make sure you request time off from work, so you can spend as much time with the kitty as possible.

In the beginning, keep the visits short and sweet. Visiting may involve directly interacting with your Siamese cat by playing with her, petting her, or quietly sitting in a chair reading a book or chatting on the phone to get her used to your presence and voice.

Keep in mind, a shy or nervous cat may hiss, growl, twitch her tail, or pull her ears back. If you notice your cat is becoming agitated, speak in a slow, low voice, and leave her alone for a while. Avoid the temptation to cuddle or pet your cat when she is upset, as it will make matters worse.

TRANSITION BEYOND THE SAFE SPACE

Once you have established a trusting relationship and good rapport with your new Siamese cat, then she is ready to start exploring the rest of the house. A word of caution: Be sure to begin the exploration process when you are home to supervise your new cat. Close the majority of the doors to bedrooms, bathroom, etc., so she can begin her exploration in stages. Too many new spaces may be overwhelming for your cat.

If you adopted a shy older cat, do not let her go into the basement or garage for several weeks. Most basements have many hiding places, often inaccessible to you. Also, make sure any doors to the outside are barricaded, preventing the older cat from bolting outside to the unknown.

Some Siamese cats quickly integrate into their new surroundings in just two or five days. However, other Siamese cats take several weeks to adapt to their new surroundings. If your Siamese cats are shy, it may take even longer.

The First Night

DO NOT let the kitten loose in the house. Make sure the kitten is in a smallish space with nowhere to hide. You might have the nicest house in the world, but it's a strange place for your new baby and the kitten will be nervous. Once the kitten is comfortable with you, leave the door open and let the kitten explore on its own terms. Just make sure it always knows where its food, water, and litter box are and can get back to them when needed.

KATHRYN BRADY
Katsmith

Kittens generally sleep eighteen to twenty hours a day, but they often do not sleep as much when introduced to a new environment. Older cats are generally more active from dawn to dusk but expect longer nights the first few nights.

The key to getting your cat to sleep is directly related to how well her sleeping arrangements match her needs. Siamese cats love to be warm and cozy. Be sure your new Siamese kitty has a secure spot to sleep that is sheltered from drafts. It is the best idea to sleep close to your kitty the first few nights, as she is used to sleeping near her littermates and mother. If possible, choose a spot off the floor, as Siamese cats love height to feel more secure and safer.

Siamese cats can see in very low light, so even with the lights turned off, your cat should be able to move around. But it may take some time for your new kitty to get accustomed to her new surroundings, so placing a nightlight in the room will make things easier on your cat in the beginning.

If you are planning on sharing your bed with your cat, you may want to wait until she is completely litter trained. If you have a kitten, it may be difficult for her to climb off the bed without hurting herself or having a potty accident. Once your cat is potty trained, she may decide to sleep with you or prefer to sprawl out on her own bed.

HOW TO GET YOUR SIAMESE CAT TO SLEEP AT NIGHT:

Play and exercise — An exhausted kitten is more likely to sleep through the entire night than an energetic one. Be sure to schedule play time an hour before bedtime, allowing your cat to burn off all that extra energy.

Change mealtimes — Sometimes, feeding your new cat a late meal can help, as cats often go to bed after eating to help digest their food. But avoid feeding a high-calorie meal just before bed time as it can promote weight gain over a long period of time.

Familiar scents — Scent is one of your Siamese cat's strongest senses. On her first night of sleeping without her littermates, she will feel overwhelmed. If the breeder gave you a small piece of a mama-scented towel or blanket, place it inside the crate to soothe your anxious little kitty.

Looking for a few other tricks to calm your new friend to sleep on her first night away from her mother?

Try hiding an old-fashioned alarm clock under her bedding. The steady tick-tock sound resembles the sound of the mama cat's heartbeat. Or try placing a hot water bottle under your cat's blanket to keep her toasty warm at night.

Your new kitten's bladder has not built up enough control to get through the entire night without needing to go to the bathroom. Make sure the litter box is within a few steps from her bed. You can slowly move it to the designated spot as your cat learns to hold her bladder.

Introducing Your Siamese Cat to Your Resident Pets

Successful introductions take time. DO NOT, and I repeat, DO NOT attempt to introduce your new cat or kitten to your resident pets upon arrival. You will permanently damage the new relationship by causing fear, anger, anxiety, and aggression. Successful relationships take time to build and cannot be rushed.

Cats

All cats have a definite personality and do not like to be forced to do anything, which is why it is so difficult to make cats like each other. Some cats embrace newcomers readily, while others learn to tolerate intruders over time. In most cases, the cats will eventually form a close bond, especially if there is no competition for food or safe sleeping places.

While it may be a matter of feline preferences as to whether your cats get along, how you introduce the new cat or kitten to the resident cat can make the difference between success or failure. Be sure to give your resident cat lots of attention so it doesn't get jealous of the newcomer. Here are some suggestions for a successful introduction.

Cat smells cat

First introductions should be sniffed out. Let scent be the first introduction, as cats sniff each other out from under the door. After two to four days, you can switch up the bedding between the new and resident cat. For example, replace your new cat's bedding with the resident cat's bedding. This is an excellent opportunity for the cats to become familiar with each other through their scents.

Once the cats stop growling and hissing at each other between the door, then you can expand the sniffing. Confine your older resident cat to a room, and then let the new cat explore the house for a couple of hours, over several days.

Cat sees cat

Once both cats are familiar with the scent of each other, then it is time to organize a meet and greet. Place your new Siamese cat into her carrier and place the carrier in the living room. Let your older resident cat freely investigate your new cat in the carrier. Both cats will be able to see and sniff each other through the carrier door.

Be sure to keep the visits short and sweet, repeating the process two or three times a day. Once the cats seem more comfortable with each other, you can lengthen the time.

If there are any signs of aggression, such as hissing or growling, retreat back into the safe room with your new cat. Be sure to reassure both cats after each trial run that you love and care for them.

Cat meets cat

Once there are no signs of aggression on either side, leave the door to the safe room open a crack. This will allow the resident cat or your new cat to explore each other's territory without feeling forced or threatened. Supervision will be required for the first few days, just in case there is some grouchy behavior.

If there are signs of aggression, have a spray bottle filled with lukewarm water. Lightly spray the cats if they begin fighting. Be alert to stop any serious signs of aggression immediately, as it may delay or damage a successful integration.

If, after a few weeks, integration is not going as smoothly as planned, consider installing an inexpensive screen door for the safe room. Each cat can take turns spending time in the safe room, and they can observe each other from behind the safety of the screen. Another option is using a natural cat pheromone diffuser to relax the cats.

Over the next few months, even years, it will be normal to observe some hissing, quarreling, swatting, and grouchy behavior. Cats are hierarchical by nature and need to establish and re-establish a pecking order within your house. Plus, like humans, cats tend to have "off" days.

Take note: The detailed time frame is purely approximate. Some integrations may be smoother and quicker than others, and others may be slower, as integration depends entirely on your cats' personalities. You know your cats best, so use common sense and a large dose of patience when integrating your new Siamese cat.

Photo Courtesy of Tammy Anderson

However, shy cats are an exception. If you have adopted a shy Siamese cat or kitten, a quicker integration may be required. Shy cats often readily welcome feline companionship and will play submissive to make the other cat accept them more readily. Often integration takes place within two to three days unless there is a health reason for keeping the cats apart longer.

Dogs

Despite the fact that dogs and cats are often portrayed as enemies, it is usually easier to introduce a new cat to a dog than to a cat. In the beginning, cats and dogs tend to be wary of each other, but they do not see each other as direct competition and, with time, can form a close bond.

Your resident dog most likely will be very excited at the aspect of introducing a new companion into his house, but he will soon settle down, as the novelty will wear off quickly. Your dog will quickly embrace the new cat or kitten as a member of his pack. Here are some suggestions for a quick and smooth integration.

Cat smells dog

Successful introductions take time and do not happen immediately. DO NOT introduce your new cat to your resident dog immediately upon arrival. By doing this, you will irreparably damage any hope of a friendly relationship in the future.

First introductions should be sniffed out.

Place your new cat in a safe room with a door that closes. Let scent be the first introduction, as the dog and the cat sniff each other out from under the door. After two to four days, you can switch up the bedding between the new cat and resident dog. For example, replace your new cat's bedding with the resident dog's bedding. This is an excellent opportunity for the feline and the canine to become familiar to each other through their scents.

Switch spots

Once the pets stop growling, barking, or hissing at each other from under the door, then you can expand the sniffing. Switch spots. Place your resident dog inside of the cat's safe room and let your new Siamese cat roam about the house for a few hours. Do this for two to three days or until your cat seems comfortable and familiar with her new surroundings.

Cat meets dog

First visual encounter – Once your Siamese cat is familiar with her new home, put your resident dog on a leash and be sure to have a handful of doggy treats in your pocket. If possible, have a family member sit near your cat on one side of the room while you stand on the other side of the room with your dog on the leash. Keep the cat and dog distracted so they do not pay too much attention to each other and get used to being in the same space.

Sit and greet – Have your resident dog sit. Help him focus on you as the leader by enticing him with a toy. If the dog accepts the toy, reward him with a treat. If your pooch tries to move toward your cat, gently pull his leash and tell him to sit. Once your dog sits, reward his good behavior again with a treat. You may need to repeat this exercise several times before your dog understands that your new cat is not prey and cannot be chased. Once your dog begins to ignore your cat's presence, you can move on to the next level.

Watch – Once your resident dog behaves himself on a leash, you can attempt taking the leash off your dog. Never leave the dog and cat unsupervised until you are absolutely sure they have built up a mutual and trusting relationship.

Cats and dogs are both hierarchical by nature, so there is no need to be surprised by the occasional swatting, growling, hissing, or grouchy behavior over the next few months.

Make sure your Siamese cat has access to a safe place for alone time. Even though your pets seem to be tolerating each other, your cat will like the option to retreat to a safe place to rest. Place a baby gate across the doorway of your cat's safe room to prevent your dog from going in the room, or buy a tall cat tower.

Integrating cats and dogs can take a few days or several weeks, as time varies depending on past experiences the dog had with cats or vice versa. Often when cats and dogs are used to being around other species, integration can be smoother and quicker.

A word about kittens and puppies

Since kittens are small, they can easily be injured by a rambunctious, energetic puppy. However, a frightened kitten can also easily harm a puppy with its claws and sharp teeth. The most important thing when introducing your kitten is her safety and the puppy's. Be sure to take things slowly, concentrating on the needs of each individual pet and never leaving them unsupervised, even for a minute or two.

Other Pets

Cats are natural-born hunters. Even though Siamese cats are typically indoor cats, they are still predators and enjoy the hunt as much as their wild relatives. There is no way to guarantee safety when you place a natural predator and prey together, but there are some ways you can minimize the danger.

Introductions

Introduce your kitty to the smaller house pet. Allow your cat to sniff your feathered or furry pets in a non-threatening manner while the animal is still in its cage. If your cat tries to swat or exhibits any type of aggressive behavior, make sure you use a strong "No" to let her know that this type of behavior is unacceptable. Never use any form of physical punishment.

Supervise

Never leave your small pets alone with your cat unsupervised. Even the most laid-back cat may decide to pounce in a lapse of judgment when she sees a little chick strutting around or a small rabbit hopping by. Stay close to make sure your Siamese cat remembers this small animal is a family friend and not food.

Never give your Siamese cat toys to play with that resembles the smaller pet. For example, never let your feline friend play with feathered toys if you have a pet bird or a stuffed squeaky mouse if you have a hamster. If your cat thinks it is okay to play with a similar toy, she most likely will assume it is okay to play with your small pets when you are not watching.

Invest in a small squirt bottle. Whenever you notice your Siamese cat approaching the small animal or cage, squirt her. Cats hate to be squirted with water, and they will quickly learn to stay away. It is also important to teach smaller children that the two pets should never play together, and they need to tightly close the lid of the cage after feeding or playing with the smaller pet. One lapse in judgment could result in a tasty treat for your cat.

A safe cage

Your smaller pets, such as rabbits, chicks, or rodents, should be placed in a safe cage that your cat cannot knock over or reach into with her paws. Beware — if your smaller pet feels threatened, these feelings can cause extreme stress that could result in the animal's death. Be sure to invest in a heavier stainless-steel cage with spacing no more than .5 inches between bars.

Fishing is a no-no

If you have a fish tank at home, your Siamese cat will most likely spend hours observing what is swimming inside of it. Your fish tank can be a nice distraction for your cat, but it can quickly turn into a problem if she decides to start fishing in it. Siamese cats are very crafty and will look for a way to unlatch the tank lid. Be sure the lid is firmly attached, as it can be dangerous if your cat accidentally falls into the tank, plus make a big mess to clean up. Never use fishbowls, as the temptation is too great for the cat's curiosity.

Photo Courtesy of Emily Miller

First Vet Visit

Once you have found a veterinarian who you feel comfortable working with, book an appointment for a meet and greet for your Siamese cat before her actual visit for her vaccines.

Any reputable veterinarian will be extremely busy and will not have time for drop-ins unless it is an emergency. Therefore, make an appointment and arrive early, so your Siamese can get used to the clinic's scents, noises, and surroundings. Often the veterinarian will recommend the meet and greet take place early in the day (maybe just when the clinic opens), as they can then control how many animals are in the waiting room.

This will allow your kitten to associate positive memories with the veterinarian's office. The employees may slip your Siamese cat a treat or two. Many pet owners who skip this step end up with cats who are absolutely petrified of going to the vet's office.

Even the calmest cat can become stressed out by a trip to the vet. A traveling case, car travel, strange noises, and scents can all increase your cat's stress levels. Fortunately, there are a few things you can do to make the experience less traumatic for you, your cat, and the vet staff.

Assemble all your cat's paperwork. Whether your cat was purchased or adopted, there will be paperwork. Your vet will want to review your cat's health records, including vaccination history, to develop a comprehensive healthcare plan. Often, your veterinarian will request photocopies of any paperwork, so be sure to make copies before heading to the vet's clinic.

Get your cat accustomed to being handled. Your vet will perform a routine physical exam of your cat. The more accustomed your kitty is to being touched and poked, the more likely she will tolerate being handled by the vet and the vet staff.

Acclimate your cat to the travel crate. Going inside the carrier can be stressful for your cat, as cats typically do not like to be confined. To ease the transition, leave the carrier open and place a few treats inside. Let your cat examine the crate and enter it of her own accord before going to the vet's office. The more familiar your cat is with the carrier, the less stressful the trip will be.

Take a practice car ride. If your feline friend is jittery about car rides, place your cat inside of her carrier and take her for a short trip around the block in the car. When you return home, take your cat out of the travel crate and praise her with some yummy rewards. Acclimating your cat to travel will reduce stress, and a calm cat is far easier for you and your vet to handle.

WHAT SHOULD YOU EXPECT DURING THE FIRST VET'S VISIT?

You will be allowed into the examination room with your Siamese kitty. Be sure to bring along some of her favorite treats. Be calm and relaxed. While talking to your cat, use an upbeat, happy voice, praising her good behavior.

The veterinarian will weigh your Siamese cat, check her temperature through her rectum, examine her eyes, ears, mouth, paws, teeth, genital region, and fur. Then the vet will listen to your cat's heartbeat and lungs using a stethoscope. The veterinarian will palpate your kitten's lymph nodes and abdominal areas. Once the general examination is finished, the vet will administer any vaccinations and de-wormers required. For more information about vaccinations and de-wormers, see Chapter 12 of this book.

The vet will most likely discuss any future medical procedures your Siamese cat might need, such as spaying or neutering and microchipping. If you have any questions regarding your cat's general health, now would be a good time to ask. Your veterinarian will give you a vaccine schedule for your Siamese cat. Be sure to place future dates on your calendar so you don't forget.

CHAPTER 5

Caring for Your Siamese Cat

Your cat's emotional and physical needs will vary depending on her age, personality, and lifestyle. Since your Siamese cat will be spending the majority of her time indoors, she will rely more heavily on you for her cat care and emotional well-being. Keeping your intelligent and emotionally sophisticated Siamese cat happy requires effort and imagination on your part.

Emotional Needs

Your furry friend's purr and endearing chin rubs are more than enough proof that she experiences a wide range of emotions. Your Siamese cat may not experience the wide range of human emotions, but she does have real emotions that motivate her behavior, such as love, appreciation, fear, and anxiety.

Cats show affection — and not just when it is dinnertime. Unless your Siamese cat has had a traumatic past with humans, she will seek you out for affection in the form of stroking, playing, or perhaps a little chit-chat about her day's events.

Siamese cats show love and affection on their own terms. For example, if a mother hugs her child, and the child happily hugs his mother back but then squirms out of her arms, that is not a sign the child is unaffectionate— it just means the child has had enough affection for now. Cats are like people, and they have boundaries.

You will discover your Siamese cat will form a strong attachment to you and your family. There are many cases where a cat owner has died and the cat shows physical and emotional signs of distress. There are stories of cats sitting at their deceased owner's door, meowing incessantly. Or they go into hiding, or they refuse to eat. In extreme cases, a perfectly healthy cat has had such a strong attachment to its owner that it dies of heartbreak after the owner passes away.

On a less dramatic note, many Siamese cat owners state that their cat knows when they are sad, depressed, or upset and will comfort them. The moral of the story is those who give love and devotion to their cats get the same in return. Sometimes much, much more.

As your Siamese cat's new guardian and friend, you have an obligation to make her life as full as possible. Here are some aspects to consider in providing for your kitty's emotional well-being.

A safe retreat

Siamese cats prefer to rest in places where they feel safe. Siamese cats may be energetic, but they love to sleep and may feel vulnerable while sleeping, especially if there are other pets in the house. Give your cat a place that is hidden away or a perch above the window so she can observe her surroundings from high up.

Opportunity to climb and scratch

Siamese cats have an innate desire to climb and scratch. Cats mark their territory with the scent glands on their paws. I cannot stress enough the

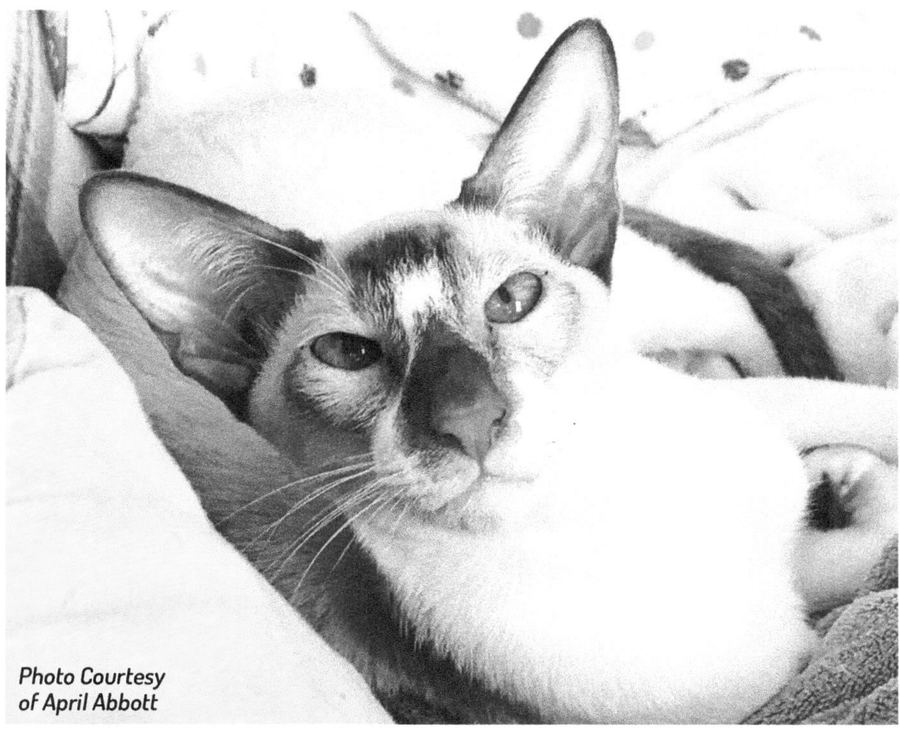

Photo Courtesy of April Abbott

importance of providing your cat with a durable and appropriate scratching option; otherwise, she will end up scratching your furniture or carpets. Siamese cats also need an opportunity to climb, as they feel safer in high places, and climbing helps them stretch their muscles.

Environmental enrichment

Siamese cats are extremely intelligent and complex. They are built for speed and stealth. A happy cat is one that can use her brain as well as her brawn. Be sure to purchase a variety of toys for your kitty to stimulate thought and also promote physical exercise.

Family bonding

You are your Siamese cat's entire world and family. In the wild, cats bond with each other by grooming and playing together. Be sure to dedicate time each day to your kitty by playing and grooming her.

Any effort you make to make to entertain and enrich your furry friend's life is worth it. Try to put yourself in your cat's paws and ask yourself what you would like if you were a cat. Never stop cherishing your amazing little furry friend.

Photo Courtesy of Nausheen Kasmani

Understanding Cat Language and Behavior

Cats rarely vocalize with other cats, except for the occasional hiss or growl. Our feline friends tend to reserve their verbal interactions for their human family. Siamese cats are extremely vocal and will use a complex mix of facial expressions, tail positions, ear positions, and sounds.

Your Siamese cat will make demands or tell you about her day by observing which of her sounds causes the desired human response. Be sure to observe the body language your cat uses when vocalizing her demands or thoughts.

Siamese cats have about a hundred words in their vocabulary in the form of meows, growls, purrs, and hisses. Pay close attention to the sounds she makes, and soon you will be able to tell when she is hungry, angry, fearful, and so on.

The following are common Siamese cat vocalizations:

- A short, quick meow means a simple, "Hello, how are you?"
- Multiple meows are your cat's way of saying, "I am so happy to see you! I have missed you!"
- A mid-pitched meow is a plea for something, usually dinner treats or water from the bathroom sink.
- A drawn-out meow is your cat's way of reminding you to do something, such as feed her dinner or clean out her litter box.
- A high-pitched meow means you accidentally stepped on your cat's tail or shut the door on her, and she wants in.
- Purring is often a sign of happiness, but a cat may purr when in pain, as it is an instinct to conceal pain from predators.
- Clicking or chirping noises mean your cat is tracking prey, such as a pesky fly, or talking to the bird on the other side of the window.

Siamese cats often use their long tail to express how they are feeling. Here are some tail movements that show how your kitty is feeling:

- Tail sticking straight up in the air with a little curl at the end means your cat is happy and in a good mood.
- A twitching tail can mean your kitty is excited or anxious.
- A vibrating tail is an indication your kitty is happy to see you.
- A tail is held low but with the tail hair sticking up is a sign of aggression.
- The tail fur sticking straight up and the tail curled under the rear is a sign the cat is scared.

Your furry friend's eyes can express her feelings. For example, slowly blinking eyes are her way of telling you she loves you. However, dilated pupils can be an indication your cat wants to play or be aggressive.

By observing your cat's face, you will be able to interpret her body language. For example, if your cat's ears are pinned back against her head, it is a sign of fear or aggression. Or, if your kitty rubs her head, body, and tail against a person or animal, it is a friendly greeting, a thank you, or an ownership claim. Another gesture that your cat will use is butting her head up against you to tell you how much she loves you.

One of the most endearing gestures your cat can use is a wet-nose kiss or lick. Or maybe it is a hint that you need to clean up after snacking on that can of sardines.

WHY DOES MY CAT MEOW AT NIGHT?

Here are some common reasons why your feline friend becomes more vocal during the wee night hours.

Cats are nocturnal

All cats, especially Siamese, are more active during certain hours of the night. Even though Siamese cats are crepuscular, which means they are most active from dusk to dawn, they often adapt to their owner's schedule. This crepuscular tendency means your cat will mostly be active early in the morning when the rest of the household sleeps.

The younger your Siamese cat is, the more active she will be at night, as her instincts kick in and tell her this is the best time to hunt. However, as your kitten matures, her routine will adapt to the rest of the household, which will mean less yowling at night.

Lack of mental stimulation or boredom

Siamese cats are very intelligent and can easily become bored. Active playtime just before bedtime may help to burn off some of your feline friend's extra energy, as will keeping her mind stimulated throughout the day.

Often, cat meowing at nighttime is attention-seeking behavior. It is vital to attend to your kitty's emotional needs, but constantly attending to her every meow may lead to her meowing even more frequently.

A sign of overactive thyroid or kidney disease

If your feline friend is frequently meowing at night, it might be a good idea to get her checked out by your veterinarian for any underlying health issues. Often, excessive vocalization at nighttime is an indication of an overactive thyroid or kidney disease.

A sign of aging

As your Siamese cat ages, she may become disoriented at night and start meowing as if she is frightened or lost. Cognitive dysfunction syndrome (CDS) directly affects the cat's brain, causing a long list of symptoms, one of which is meowing at night.

Photo Courtesy of Simone Moller

Mating call

Yowling at night may be a sound of mating. Mating is a natural process, which is one of the reasons why I strongly recommend getting your cat neutered or spayed. It significantly reduces your cat's loud yowling noises at night.

Be sure to get your veterinarian to check your kitty to make sure there is nothing physically wrong with her. Your vet will most likely give you more advice on how to prevent your furry friend from meowing at night.

Why do Cats Purr?

Purring is one of the most common sounds your Siamese cat will make. But we should not assume that the sound of purring just means the cat is in a good mood. Cats purr to communicate other emotions besides contentment.

Happiness – If your cat looks happy and she is purring, then it is safe to assume she is in a happy place. Just consider the purr a big smile telling you how happy she is.

Hungry – Some Siamese cats purr when they are hungry or it's mealtime. Once you get to know your cat, you should be able to distinguish between a purr of happiness or purr/cry of hungry.

Connection – Kittens start purring when they are only a few days old to let their mothers know they are safe and where they are. A mother cat purrs to her kittens to tranquilize them; often, it is called the mother cat's lullaby. If your cat purrs when you pick her up or caress her, take it as a compliment that she feels connected to you.

Relief and healing – Often, a cat will purr when she is hurt or in pain. Recent research suggests that purring helps the cat feel better faster. The low frequency and vibrations of purring can help heal wounds and bones. Plus, it can help to build muscle, repair tendons, and calm pain and swelling.

Preventing Hairballs

There is no denying the truth — cat hairballs are unpleasant. Hairballs are not only disgusting to clean up, but they can cause blockages in your cat's intestines, leading to serious health problems. Your Siamese cat is an avid groomer, so how can you keep hairballs to a minimum?

Photo Courtesy of Cait & Del Burns

WHAT CAUSES HAIRBALLS?

Hairballs are a direct result of your Siamese cat's fastidious and healthy grooming routine. When your cat grooms herself, the tiny hook-like structures on her tongue catch the loose, dead hair, which is often swallowed. The majority of hair will easily pass through the digestive tract with no issues. But if the hair becomes trapped in the stomach, it will form into a hairball. Normally, your cat will gag on the hairball until she vomits it up on your carpet.

Hairballs often are not round. Instead, they are thin and tube-shaped after passing through the narrow esophagus.

Siamese cats are prone to hairballs because they groom themselves compulsively, and they tend to swallow a lot of fur. It is not common for kittens to have hairballs as they are not adept groomers yet. As your cat ages, she will become more proficient at removing dead, loose hair from her coat with her tongue, meaning more hairballs for you to clean up.

SYMPTOMS OF HAIRBALLS

It can be quite distressing to hear (and see) your kitty cough up a hairball. Some common symptoms of an emerging hairball are hacking, retching, and gagging, all of which are followed by your cat vomiting up the hairball.

If you notice any of the following symptoms, be sure to contact your veterinarian immediately, as it may be an indication of a hairball blockage:

- Ongoing vomiting, gagging, retching, or hacking without producing a hairball
- Lack of appetite
- Diarrhea or constipation
- Lethargy

FUN FACT

Hypoallergenic?

With their fluffy cream-colored coats, you might not expect Siamese cats to be hypoallergenic, but they do fall into this category. While Siamese cats are not the most hypoallergenic breed—this distinction falls to the hairless Sphynx—many people with mild to moderate allergies are well suited to this breed. But how can such a fluffy cat be hypoallergenic? Siamese cats simply produce less of the allergy-inducing Fel d 1 protein in their saliva than other breeds!

HOW TO PREVENT HAIRBALLS

It is impossible to completely eliminate hairballs, but there are a few things you can do to reduce the frequency.

Groom your Siamese cat regularly

The more fur you remove from your kitty while brushing, the less fur will end up as a hairball in her stomach. Brushing your kitty daily is one of the most effective ways of minimizing hairballs. Siamese cats generally love to be brushed, but in case your cat is the exception and you cannot get her accustomed to brushing, then consider taking her to a professional groomer every two to three months.

Use specialized "hairball formula" cat food

Many pet food manufacturers make cat food that aids in reducing the buildup of hairballs. These formulas are often higher in fiber and designed to improve your cat's coat health, minimize shedding, and aid hairballs in passing through the digestive tract.

Use hairball laxatives

There are a variety of hairball laxative products available at the local pet supply store. These laxatives are very mild and are designed to encourage the cat to pass the hairball through the digestive tract. Be sure to read the reviews on each product before choosing the best option for your cat.

Discourage excessive grooming

If you suspect your Siamese cat's hairballs are the result of excessive grooming, try enticing your cat into another activity. Often, a bored cat will develop the habit of compulsive grooming. Make sure your kitty has plenty of toys to keep her mentally stimulated.

Photo Courtesy of Becky Brown

Mental Stimulation

One thing that I recommend is playing at least once a day with your Siamese. Much like dogs, cats need interaction and playtime. In these moments of playtime, you can teach the cat to play fetch. Another way to keep your Siamese healthy and active is to get a running water bowl. Cats will drink more water if the water is moving and not still.

AMANDA WILLIAMS
AW Cattery

You will want to make sure you keep your Siamese cat busy with plenty of activities. Siamese need to stretch their brains to prevent boredom. Otherwise, they may become destructive or start getting into things they shouldn't.

With a little creativity, you will be able to keep your furry friend entertained for hours, even in a small apartment or on a limited budget. Here are some creative ways to stimulate your Siamese cat so she does not get bored and start misbehaving.

Foraging fun

Instead of just feeding your feline friend out of the bowl, why not appeal to her inner hunter by hiding pieces of kibble around the house? Place a few pieces of kibble in your cat's favorite napping spot so she will find them. This activity will encourage foraging and prevent her from scarfing down her food too quickly. If you have a dog, make sure the kibble is out of his reach; otherwise, he will gobble it up.

Bird watching

If possible, attach a suction cup bird feeder outside your cat's favorite window. Your Siamese cat will spend hours watching the hungry birds munch away on seeds. Just a word of caution: Make sure the windows are tightly closed, as an excited cat can push her way through the screen.

Late-night games

Siamese cats are nocturnal, so look for glow-in-the-dark toys that will spark your cat's curiosity. Some toys have lights that are motion-activated or contain catnip. If you are a light sleeper, be sure to put away any of your cat's toys that have disruptive noisemakers; otherwise, your cat will keep you awake throughout the night.

Interactive toys and puzzles

From teaser feather toys to interactive track toys, you will be able to keep your curious kitty busy for hours, providing her with the mental stimulation she needs by channeling her hunting instincts. Look for games that get your kitty physically involved by swatting, batting, chasing and catching a ball, feather, or a squeaky mouse. Puzzles are another excellent way to engage your kitten and boost her happiness level.

Scratchers

Every Siamese cat needs a scratcher. Cats stretch out their paws to leave their scent, as their scent glands are in their paws. Also, cats love to scratch because it helps them stretch out and relax. Another interesting fact about stretching is that it helps to get rid of the dead skin on their paws.

Play together

Purchase a board game such as feline cards or dominos, which allows you to place one or two pieces of kibble or yummy treats in some of the game parts. Give your Siamese cat one of the many toys with a hidden treat and let her try to figure out how to work it out. Another option is to play hide-and-seek or do a treasure hunt.

Cardboard boxes

Siamese cats love to play in boxes. Your cat will literally spend hours jumping in and out, sliding around inside, or using the box to play hide and seek. A simple cardboard box is an easy way to keep your feline friend entertained for hours. The box might be destroyed after a day or two, but they are easy and cheap to replace.

Switch up your kitty's toy collection

Nobody wants to play with the same old toy day after day. Give your Siamese cat a toy to play with and when she becomes bored with it, replace it with another one. Keep all of her toys in a box and rotate them out. Your cat will love it when you switch up her toys and will feel as if she is getting a brand-new toy.

Options if Your Pets Don't Get Along

Every pet owner's secret dream is to come home and find their pets cuddled up together on the couch. Unfortunately, pets do not always get along, especially if they are different species. If you find your pets cannot be friendly, keep them separated for a few days, then reintroduce them to each other.

REASONS WHY PETS MAY NOT GET ALONG:

Hormonal – Many disagreements between pets often are related to hormonal changes. An easy fix for this problem is to make sure that all of your resident pets are neutered or spayed, as this will keep any aggression at bay.

Food – All animals, no matter their species, have a built-in instinct to protect their food. If your pets tend to become aggressive around mealtimes, place your pets' food dishes in separate parts of the house and feed them at the same time.

Jealousy – All pets need to feel loved and cherished. An easy solution for this problem is to designate quality time with each of your pets alone, without the other pets watching. This will ensure each pet that you love it and will never replace it.

Dominance – Rivalry among pets is normal, especially if you bring a new pet into the household. Only one pet can be the leader of the pack, and this is something they need to figure out on their own terms and time schedule. Once your pets have established which pet is the leader, respect their decision by feeding the boss first.

A good relationship between your pets may take a few days to establish, or it may take a couple of years. Fights will happen, especially during the first few weeks, as they determine who will be the dominant leader in your house. One way to make your animals back off from fighting is to douse them in water — trust me, they will back off immediately.

If you fear your pets' behavior towards each other may cause them harm, it is not unreasonable to think about giving up one of your pets. Some pets cannot and will not tolerate other pets and are happier living in an "only child" environment.

But, before you consider such a drastic decision, there are lots of behavior specialists out there who are willing to extend a helping hand to encourage your pets to get along. A certified pet trainer or a board-certified veterinary behaviorist will be able to diagnose and treat your pets' stress, anxiety, phobias, aggression, and reactivity toward each other. Often extreme misbehavior occurs because the pet is suffering from an underlying medical condition, so be sure to check with your vet.

Ask around

Perhaps you have come to the difficult decision to give up one of your pets. If so, first ask a friend or family member if they would like to adopt your pet. If you ask around, you will be pleasantly surprised how many people would be thrilled to give your pet a new forever home. Just make sure the home is suitable for your pet by visiting ahead of time.

If you did not have luck with the above alternatives, then contact pet trainers or your veterinarian to see if they know of any good homes that are searching for a good pet.

Seek out rescue groups

Most localities have active rescue groups dedicated to "fostering" pets in a caring home until they can find them their forever home. One of the main advantages of a rescue group is you are assured that your pet is going into the home of someone who not only loves pets but understands how to take care of them. There is also the option of looking for rescue breed-specific groups. If you are considering surrendering your pet to a shelter, you need to make sure it is a no-kill facility.

CHAPTER 6

Laying a Solid Foundation for Training Your Siamese Cat

> *Siamese are very smart and curious! I have taught mine to fetch, sit, lie down, and roll over. They can be harness-taught for going on walks. Being curious, they will explore every inch of their environment!*
>
> KAREN SPOHN
>
> *Candi Dasa cattery*

Siamese cats are enchanting, but let's be honest — raising a kitten is not without its challenges. Nonetheless, there is no turning back once those big blue eyes capture your heart! In this chapter, we will discuss how to help your Siamese cat grow into a happy, healthy, and well-adjusted cat.

Importance of Socialization

All Siamese cats require early socialization in order to be good pets. Socialization teaches kittens how to properly interact with other cats, animals, and people. However, these interactions need to be positive experiences; otherwise, your cat will be traumatized and fearful of similar encounters in the future.

A properly socialized cat will be confident and secure in its home environment. In a sense, taking the time to socialize your cat while she is still a kitten is like giving her emotional health insurance that will stay with her throughout all of her nine lives.

Your Siamese cat can be socialized at any age as they continue to learn throughout their long lives. However, kittens are easier to train than older cats. If you adopted an older Siamese cat, be sure to follow the suggestions in this chapter but at a slower pace and with more frequent repetition.

Photo Courtesy of Emelia Harewood

FUN FACT
A Cat That Talks

Siamese cats are one of the most vocal cat breeds. This need to speak is most likely caused by the Siamese cat's social and outgoing nature. These cats enjoy interacting with their humans and require more attention than some other cat breeds. Vocalization is another way Siamese cats communicate with their humans. Over time, you may learn to distinguish between different sounds that your cat makes and even begin to understand what these various vocalizations mean!

Siamese kittens are like furry sponges that absorb everything around them — including the good and the bad. The prime time to socialize a cat is between two and seven weeks of age. Your cat's mother, littermates, and breeder will have an impact on her personality. For example, a kitten who is not exposed to a positive experience with humans during this short period of time may grow up to be a shy cat and may never feel comfortable around people.

Proper socialization teaches your kitty how to act like a cat, proper feline manners, how to clean herself, how to communicate with other felines, and who is a friend and who is not. Most of these early socialization skills should be learned by the time you bring your Siamese kitten home.

COPYCATS

There is a good reason why people use the term — copycats! Kittens learn everything by copying their mother and imitating her behavior. If the mother cat is friendly with the household dog, then her kittens will generally accept dogs as safe friends. But if the mother cat reacts hysterically when she sees a dog, then the kitten will most likely react the same way.

Kittens learn proper claw and biting etiquette with their littermates. Interactions with each other and adult cats help your kitten learn to use kitty language with fluffed fur and tails, meows, howls, and body language. For this reason, it is ideal for the kitten to stay with her mother and littermates as long as possible — ten to twelve weeks at least.

Many behavioral issues stem from unfamiliar situations. Simple things such as rearranging the furniture can be stressful for a cat. You can help your kitten be more forgiving of these changes by introducing these types of changes frequently when she is younger. Move the furniture, provide a wide assortment of toys and hiding spots regularly, and introduce your kitten to people as much as possible.

Photo Courtesy of C.A Beber

How to Socialize Your Siamese

You just brought home your Siamese cat. You are having a wonderful time playing with her, cuddling with her, and showing her off to friends and family. Whether you are aware of it or not, these are all important aspects of socializing your feline friend. However, the more you can intentionally tailor your interactions with your cat while she is young, the more well-adjusted she will be when she grows up.

Here are some suggestions of how to socialize your Siamese kitten or older cat:

- **Hold, touch, and cuddle your kitty as much as possible** — Be sure to touch her ears, paws, nails, tail, tummy, mouth, and under her chin as cats can be uncomfortable being touched in those areas.
- **Practice placing your cat in a travel carrier and going for short car rides** — Older cats often dislike leaving their familiar surroundings and associate car rides with a trip to the vet.
- **Play together frequently** — One of the best ways to teach your kitty positive behavior is by playing together. Never allow your cat to play with strings or ribbons, as she can easily swallow them, resulting in serious health issues.
- **Get your Siamese cat used to noise** — Play soft music in your house. Personally, I find my Siamese cats love piano music. Use the vacuum or the hair dryer frequently in your cat's presence.
- **Search out a kitten class** — Finding a kitten class might be a little more difficult than a puppy class. Be sure to check with your veterinarian or groomer to see if they know of any in your area.

Since it is difficult to take your Siamese cat out of her comfort zone, you will have to bring new situations to her. When introducing a new person or animal, make sure you are relaxed and calm, as your cat can read your emotions. If you are nervous, then your furry friend will be nervous too, and perhaps even afraid of the new situation.

Remember, Rome was not built in a day — take your time introducing your Siamese cat to everyone on your list. Start off slow, first with friends and family, then integrate a stranger, such as the postman.

Before introducing your Siamese cat to somebody new, inform them ahead of time that the purpose of the visit is a brief socialization session for your kitty. Ask them to be ready to pamper her with love and affection, and be sure to slip your guests a treat or two to give your cat.

Photo Courtesy of Sheryl Langdon

Start off with meeting people in neutral, familiar environments, not a get-together with music or a party, which can be overwhelming for you and your kitty. Instead, plan your meet and greet in your kitchen or living room. Once your Siamese cat is comfortable with these situations, you can try inviting a few more people over.

Here are some helpful suggestions to help your Siamese become acclimated to all sorts of people:

- Stay calm and confident during meet and greets, and even more so if your Siamese cat is frightened. If your cat is skittish or agitated, don't make a big deal about her behavior, as it will cause her to become more upset.
- When asking a stranger to pat your Siamese cat, ask them to pat her where their hands can be seen, such as her chest or under her chin.
- Use treats and praise to give your Siamese cat a positive association with meeting strangers and experiencing new situations.
- Enlist a different cat sitter each week to expose your Siamese cat to a variety of caregivers during the day.

Your Siamese cat should be exposed to the following people within her first few months with you:

- Neighbors
- Family and friends
- Groomer and vet
- Unfamiliar people wearing different styles of clothes (hoods, jackets, face masks, sunglasses, uniform, hats, and so on)
- Postman
- Anyone who regularly comes to your house

When socializing your Siamese cat or kitten, remember that positivity is the key. Make sure that all of the activities and interactions leave a positive impression on your feline friend. If she shows any sign of fear, aggression, or reluctance, slow down and increase the distance between her and the object, pet, or person.

Never punish your cat by hitting or yelling at her if she does not respond to the new situation the way you planned. That is a surefire way to get her to develop long-lasting negative associations with that object and you.

TIPS FOR SOCIALIZING AN OLDER SIAMESE CAT

If you have adopted or rescued an older Siamese cat that is not well-socialized or needs to brush up on her social skills, here is everything you need to know:

Siamese cats have an independent spirit and easily become set in their ways as they age, making them particularly affected by change. But with patience and time, you can help the most stubborn cat become more confident and friendly with people.

Your adopted cat may never come to trust strange animals but may be able to tolerate them from a safe distance. If you want to introduce your older cat to a new pet, please follow the details in Chapter 4 of this book.

It is important to understand why an older cat can be apprehensive and uncomfortable in social situations.

- Events related to people or certain animals in the cat's past might have been painful or traumatic.
- Your cat could have a shy disposition from birth.
- There might have been a lack of socialization with people and other animals when the cat was still a kitten.
- The cat was separated from her mother too soon before proper socialization with littermates could take place.

Here are some suggestions to help an older cat learn to feel more comfortable around people:

Host a low-key gathering — Invite one or two cat-loving people who have calm demeanors over to your house. Give your friends a handful of your cat's favorite treats as they come into the house. Tell your friends to ignore your feline friend unless she comes to them to investigate. If she does, they can speak in a calm voice and give her a treat or two. If your cat keeps a distance, your friends can toss her a treat occasionally, so she associates new people with yummy treats.

Use a small room — Shy cats can be overwhelmed by too much space, and they will feel safer in a smaller area. Be sure there are plenty of hiding spots throughout the room, such as boxes, under the couch, tables, and high spots to observe your guests from a safe distance.

Use pheromones — Pheromones are substances that mimic the calming scent that a mother makes to help relax her kittens. It comes in many different forms, such as a spray or diffuser, and can go a long way in helping a shy cat feel more comfortable about interacting.

Remember, the two essential things to keep in mind to help an older cat learn to trust people are that it will take time, and you should always be patient and kind.

Stop Unruly Behavior from Day One

All cats are stubborn; that's one of the reasons we love them so much. Be firm. If the kitty is clawing the rug, say 'NO!' loudly and firmly, but don't scream. Then get up (no matter how comfortable you might be) and show the kitten where it is supposed to scratch; put the kitty gently on its scratching post. It's a natural behavior, so you can't stop it, but you can modify it. Siamese have long bodies, so make sure the scratching post is tall enough and heavily weighted at the bottom. Don't punish a cat; just give it an option for behavior that is acceptable to you.

KATHRYN BRADY
Katsmith

Siamese cats are known for jumping on the kitchen counters, chewing on wires, and scratching items that are not meant to be scratched. Many of these undesirable traits are the cat's natural reaction to the environment, but others are just bad habits.

Allowing your cat to behave poorly without consequences will only reinforce the idea that the behavior is acceptable. Fortunately, it is possible to change your kitty's behavior by rewarding her good behavior and disciplining her for unacceptable behavior. However, you do not want to permanently damage your relationship with your cat or physically hurt her. So, it is vital you learn how to discipline your feline friend correctly.

TRAIN YOUR CAT

Siamese cats are probably one of the easiest cats to train due to their intelligence and great memory. According to experts, Siamese cats have both long-term and short-term memory making them highly trainable. But at the same time, this means they know what they can get away with again and again if there are no consequences.

Cats, like dogs, react well to positive reinforcement, so generally, they will remember when they get a yummy treat or generous praise from their human family. Siamese cats thrive on attention, toys, and yummy snacks. Choose the most desirable item for training, and only use this item for positive reinforcement. By reserving this item for training, it will add to the value of the reward, making that much more enticing to your cat.

If your kitten is fussy, consider enticing her with pieces of tuna, shrimp, or catnip toys. You may need to mix them up a bit if your cat loses interest.

DISCOURAGE BAD BEHAVIOR

Cats are more receptive to a tasty reward than they are to punishment. But there are a few ways to discourage bad behavior:

Shake a noisy can – If your cat jumps up on the table or kitchen counter or anywhere else she is not allowed to be, shake a can with some loose change in it to startle your furry friend. You will need to repeat the process until she associates the place with strange noises.

Use scent deterrents – Siamese cats tend to dislike citrus smells and red pepper flakes. Also, there are a variety of cat deterrent sprays with a bitter taste or smell to deter your cat from scratching or chewing on certain things. Be sure to follow the instructions on the bottle to avoid discoloration of the fabric or carpet.

Use a water spray bottle – Cats hate being squirted with water. Give your kitty a quick squirt of water if she is wandering somewhere or doing something she should not. Most likely, after a few squirts, just reaching for the water bottle will deter your cat from doing the bad behavior.

Give a timeout – If your Siamese cat is misbehaving, gently place her in a neutral place with no people in it for at least twenty minutes. Quite often, your cat will emerge from the room with a completely different attitude.

Say something – Startle your cat with a loud "no" or "ouch" to put a stop to any rough behavior. This method is effective if your cat is aggressive with strangers or likes to chase after you and bite or grab your leg.

Use different textures – Cats are wary of strange textures such as double-sided tape or aluminum foil. These simple things can be placed near to or on the surface of something you do not want your cat scratching.

NEVER USE HARSH DISCIPLINE

Studies have proven that using harsh discipline in cat training is counterproductive. In general, Siamese cats respond better to training when combined with positive reinforcement like praise and treats. Harsh discipline involves yelling, hitting, use of physical force, grabbing at the scruff of the neck, and staring down. All of these negative actions will seriously affect your cat in the following ways:

- They may cause your feline friend to become aggressive.
- They may cause your Siamese cat to become fearful and suffer from separation anxiety later on in life.
- They may teach your cat to distrust humans.

When you hit or yell at your cat, you are teaching her to fear you, breaking her trust and weakening her confidence. There is no place for any type of harsh discipline in training your cat.

Never scruff your kitten or cat by the back of the neck. This is no longer a recommended method of restraining, carrying, or disciplining a cat. In the past, it was believed scruffing a cat made them relaxed, but it is fear paralysis. Scruffing is very painful for your cat, and when you cause a misbehaving cat pain, it will only make the matter a hundred times worse.

A much gentler alternative to grabbing a cat by the scruff of her neck is putting a blanket over her and scooping her up inside of it. The cat will feel safe and allow you to transport her without stressing her out further.

Rebellious or Bad Parenting?

There is an old English saying, "To err is human," which means we all make mistakes. That saying could not be truer than when it comes to teaching your Siamese cat proper behavior.

Here are some of the most common mistakes people make while training their Siamese cats.

Waiting too long to start training – Teaching your Siamese cat about the differences between good and bad behavior should begin the minute she comes home with you, regardless of whether she is a kitten or an older cat from a shelter. Avoid the temptation to wait until she outgrows her adorable kitten stage, as she will develop bad behavior and habits in the interim.

Siamese kittens should be able be able to master potty training quickly, but it may take longer for them to learn the difference between sharpening their claws on their scratching post and on your furniture.

Rewarding negative behavior – Many Siamese cat owners do not realize they are rewarding their kitten's bad behavior. For example, they might comfort their kitty because she was frightened from being left alone for a few minutes. This leads to repetition of the same unwanted behavior.

Siamese cats are very sociable felines who thrive on their owner's attention. Whenever you give your cat attention, she understands that you are pleased with her current behavior and thinks it should continue. If you notice your kitty is lying next to something she used to chew or scratch, reward her! She will quickly learn the difference between good and bad behavior.

Inconsistency – Inconsistent training will confuse your Siamese cat. For example, let's say your kitty is not allowed on the table, but occasionally you make the exception for your cat to sit on the table for a snack or two. But then you turn around and discipline your cat for jumping up on the table when you are eating dinner. She will not understand what she did wrong, as one minute she is allowed on the table and the next, she is not.

Impatient – Training your Siamese about what is expected of her takes time, and you need to remember that every cat learns at a different pace. Avoid getting frustrated while training your cat, as she will pick up on your negative vibes. Training sessions should be upbeat and positive, so make sure your attitude is in the right frame of mind first.

CAUTION: *Never discipline or train your Siamese cat when you are in a bad mood. This is a recipe for disaster. You could easily take your frustration and anger out on your poor, defenseless cat if she makes a mistake. Instead, make a cup of tea and snuggle up with your kitty on the couch until your mood improves.*

Lack of daily routine – Siamese cats love routine. During the first few months with your cat, she will learn where to eat, play, sleep and go potty. By establishing a specific routine and time schedule when these things happen, you will promote proper behavior and confidence in your cat. Siamese cats are eager to please their new family, so use this to your advantage!

Be sure to establish a manageable routine for your Siamese cat before you bring her home. This will help to avoid unnecessary stress and get your cat on the right track as soon as possible.

Picking the Right Treats

There are many ways to reward your kitten for good behavior, but nothing is better than a yummy treat! Here are some useful tips to help you choose the best reward for different situations:

Small-sized treats – When you are trying to reinforce good behavior, it is important to keep your cat motivated and attentive. In these cases, she will be eating lots of treats in a short period of time. Choose treats that are smaller and that can be quickly gobbled up.

Soft and smelly treats – All cats love soft, stinky treats. These treats are best suited for more complex situations, such as when introducing your cat to another pet or a new person. Or perhaps you want to train your Siamese cat to walk on a leash. In that case, you will need extra motivation to keep your cat focused on you and not the noises outside.

Chewy treats – For some training sessions, you need the treat to last longer, such as with crate training or learning to lie still beside you on the couch. For these occasions, use a chewy reward your cat can savor, or try using a chewing toy that can be stuffed with treats.

Switch it up – Siamese cats can become bored with a certain treat. For impromptu positive reinforcement, have a grab bag of a mix of different treats to keep your feline friend motivated. Try cutting up dried tuna treats into small pieces and add soft and hard treats to the grab bag; this will keep her intrigued.

> *Siamese are as smart as a dog and just as trainable. But, they DO NOT respond to punishment training. You must use treats and praise to be successful. Just a warning though: they will train you just as easily as you train them!*
>
> WILLIAM HARRISON
> *Kittentanz Cattery*

CAUTION: *Cat treats are high in calories and sugar. They are designed to be given as an occasional treat or reward. For this reason, it is important that whenever you give your cat treats, you reduce her main meal by an equivalent caloric amount. Never give your cat more than 10 percent of her daily caloric intake in kitty treats, as they often lack the necessary nutrients.*

Scratching the Furniture

By scratching carpets and furniture, your cat is sending out a message to the other pets in the house that this area belongs to her. Plus, scratching helps your cat relax and feel secure by stretching out her muscles.

Your cat may also simply be sharpening her claws. Claws grow constantly and quickly, and scratching helps to keep them down.

This behavior can easily be corrected by providing your cat with a scratching post. A scratching post will keep your cat entertained, and with time, she will lose interest in scratching other areas. Every time your cat uses the scratching post, her paws will release a scent to mark this territory as her own and encourage her to return the post and not your couch.

However, with use, your cat's scratching post will show wear and tear, so be sure to replace it at least once a year.

Never declaw your cat, as your cat's claws are an extension of her bones. Declawing is actually an amputation and is an extremely painful and cruel procedure. Declawing is not the same as cutting your cat's nails, and any reputable veterinarian will refuse to submit your cat to this inhumane procedure. Declawing will impact your cat's emotional health and remove her ability to defend herself.

How to prevent your cat from scratching your furniture and carpets:

- **Use textures** - Place aluminum foil or double-sided masking tape on the sides of your furniture as a deterrent for your cat.
- **Use scents** - Make a mix of equal parts water and apple cider vinegar in a spray bottle and apply to the spots your Siamese cat is damaging.
- **Use an upside-down vinyl carpet runner** - Place the spike side up in front of or on the spot your kitty loves to scratch.
- **Clap your hands loudly** - Whenever you catch your cat in the act of scratching your furniture or carpets, clap loudly, and she will stop immediately
- **Spray with water** - Whenever you catch your cat in the act of scratching your furniture or carpets, spray her with a squirt of water, and she will stop immediately.

Entice your cat to use a scratching post by sprinkling it with catnip and placing it in front of items you do not want her scratching. Some Siamese cats are fussy about textures, so you may need to experiment with scratching posts with different textures, such as corrugated cardboard, carpeting, rope, or tweed.

To further entice your cat to use her scratching post, you can use pheromones on an ongoing basis. Pheromones are available as sprays, wipes, and diffusers to help calm your cat. A calm cat means less scratching behavior caused by stress or anxiety. Another option is nail caps. Nail caps are small plastic nail coverings that are placed on your cat's nail to prevent scratching.

Biting and Chewing

Cats and kittens play by swatting, pouncing, chewing, biting, and kicking. However, sometimes, our feline friends can get too frisky with us, leaving behind bites and scratches that may become infected.

Never let your Siamese kitten play with your feet or hands by chewing on them. Kittens who grow up nibbling on fingertips often grow up into cats who bite hard. If your cat's biting and chewing have become a concern, look for the cause before finding a solution.

- Check with your vet for any dental concerns.
- Be sure you are feeding your Siamese cat a nutritionally complete cat food with a seal by the Association of American Feed Control Officials (AAFCO) on the packaging.
- Perhaps your cat is bored and needs more suitable toys to play with.
- For persistent cats that try to bite or chew on things they should not, try using bitter sprays designed for cats as a deterrent.

Consider the possibility that your cat is taking her aggression out on something by biting or chewing on it. There are a number of products geared toward decreasing a cat's stress and anxiety, such as pheromones. You can also give your cat other things to focus her energy on, such as exercise-inducing toys.

Jumping on Tables and Counters

Siamese cats love high places and are excellent jumpers. The higher the vantage point, the better, even more so if there is food nearby. In the wild, cats climb trees and leap long distances to find food and avoid danger. Therefore, it should come as no surprise that your Siamese cat engages her instincts, even if she lives indoors.

The simplest way to keep your kitty off the counters is never to place her on your counter or table. Once you allow your furry friend up on the kitchen table or counters, she will think it is proper behavior.

If your cat is jumping up on your table or counters in search of food, then try keeping them clean and free of tempting food to avoid reinforcing this undesirable behavior.

You can try using environmental deterrents, such as unpleasant smells and textures, to keep your cat away without punishing them. Environmental

Photo Courtesy of Lindsay Linklater

deterrents are less stressful than clapping your hands or squirting your cat with water. Try using one of the following methods:

- Balance a cookie sheet unevenly on your countertops so they make a scary noise when your cat jumps on them.
- Place double-sided masking around the edges of your table and counters.
- Place a plastic mat with nubs on the bottom upside down on your counters and table. The surface will feel quite unpleasant to your cat.

- Hang towels along the edge of your table and counter, so when your cat jumps up, she will slide off with the towels.

One of the best aspects of these deterrents is they do not involve you actively in scaring your cat. Avoid removing your cat from your table and counter with your hands, as she will consider the personalized attention from you a sign of approval and will only jump up again. If you scare your cat, then she might think you are scary and not the counters and table.

Environmental deterrents teach your kitty that counters and tables are scary and off-limits.

Meowing

As discussed earlier, meowing is completely normal for Siamese cats, but it can be a sign that something is wrong.

- Howling at night may be a sign of senility for older Siamese cats.
- If your cat is meowing, crying, or howling while eliminating in her litter box, it usually is a sign she is experiencing pain or discomfort.
- Vocalization may be a sign of pain, such as from a catfight with your other resident cat or a pinched tail in the door.

Providing your kitten with something to play with at night may help prevent excessive meowing. Often, having two cats will prevent night howling for attention, as they will keep each other company while you sleep. You can also give your cat more exercise during the day to ensure she is less active during the night.

Never punish your cat for meowing, as it is her only way of communicating with you.

Your cat may howl when she wants food or if her litter box is dirty. The response you give your cat, such as giving up and crawling out of bed to give her some attention, will train her to continue to make these vocalizations to get what she wants, when she wants it. If she is meowing for attention, the best thing you can do is simply ignore her.

Mounting

Mounting and humping are normal behaviors for both male and female cats. Your Siamese cat may attempt to mount moving and inert objects, such as people, other animals, cat beds, and toys, or she will just lick herself.

Neutered and spayed cats may continue mounting or humping because this behavior feels good.

SIMPLE SOLUTION

If you notice that your Siamese cat is trying to mount or hump, quickly try to distract her. Play a game or toss her a puzzle toy. Or squirt her with water. Over time, your cat will forget about this behavior, but only if you nip it in time.

Begging

Begging is a habit that your feline friend learns from you, and it is extremely difficult to break. Most Siamese cats love to eat; however, table scraps are not kitty treats and can cause a long list of digestive issues and obesity. It may seem almost impossible to resist those baby blue eyes, but giving in just once will create problematic behavior in the long run.

SIMPLE SOLUTION

Before you sit down for dinner or chow down on some pizza on the sofa, distract your cat with her favorite toy or puzzle with a treat inside. If necessary, confine your cat to another room. If she behaves, be sure to give her a treat or two after your family has completely finished eating.

Clicker Training and Cats

Siamese cats are extremely easy to train and often respond to signals rather than commands.

You probably have already trained your feline friend to come without even realizing it. For example: think about what happens when the can opener buzzes or some fresh kibble hits the bowl. Your cat comes running at lightning speed. Your Siamese cat has learned a signal, such as the sound of the can opener or a rattle in the bowl, which means if she comes, she will get something yummy.

If you start saying the word "come" every time you fill your cat's food dish, within a short period of time, she will learn what the word comes means. After this, you can start training your cat using a clicker and her favorite treats. Siamese cats can be trained to come, sit, wave a paw, sit up, and even walk on a leash.

Clickers are some of the fastest ways of creating a common language with your Siamese cat. A clicker is often combined with other positive reinforcement methods. Your Siamese cat does not know what you want her to do, so you need to mark her behavior. A clicker marks the exact behavior you approve of and want the cat to repeat.

WHAT IS A CLICKER?

A clicker is a small handheld device. It has a thin metal strip inside that makes a distinctive clicking sound whenever you push down on the button. You can find a clicker at most pet supply stores; an added bonus is that they are quite inexpensive. Cats tend to prefer a softer "snick" sound, such as a ballpoint pen. Or your cat may respond to a tongue click, which means you don't need to buy a clicker.

CAUTION: *Be careful in selecting an everyday product, such as a ballpoint pen or a regular sound, so it does not confuse your kitty with everyday noises in the house that are not signaling training.*

The clicker allows you to communicate effectively with your cat by showing her exactly what you liked about her behavior. When you ask your Siamese to sit down, the instant her butt hits the ground, activate the clicker, followed by a reward as quickly as possible.

HOW TO INTRODUCE A CLICKER:

Sit down on the floor with your cat and a bowl full of her favorite treats and begin to CLICK and toss a treat, CLICK and toss another treat. Repeat as many times as your cat shows interest. If your cat is not interested in snacks, use an enticing toy such as feathers, then CLICK and offer the feather, CLICK and offer the feather. Repeat as many times as your cat seems interested.

Be aware that your cat will not want to train for a long period of time, as they easily become bored. Your cat may simply walk away after half a dozen repeats. Do not force your cat back to the training session. It is better to have several short training sessions than a singular marathon event.

HOW TO USE THE CLICKER FOR BASIC COMMANDS:

- At the exact moment your Siamese cat completes the desired action, press the clicker. Then, reward her with a treat and with praise.

- Be aware that if you do not click at the exact moment your cat performed the new behavior, she might not associate the new action with the treat.
- For more complicated commands or tricks, you can click and reward for small steps toward the desired behavior.

A clicker will not replace high-calorie treats, but with time you will be able for wean your Siamese cat off them, as the sound of the clicker is a reward in itself. However, this does not mean you can stop using treats. You will still need to give your cat an occasional treat; otherwise, the clicker will stop being as effective.

If you have an older Siamese with teeth or weight issues, a healthier option to kitty treats is to give her a few pieces of unseasoned cooked chicken or tuna during the clicker training sessions. Remember, your cat lives in the moment, so when you click the clicker, immediately give her a treat, so she can learn to associate the clicking sound with a treat.

Test your Siamese cat when she is playing or distracted by clicking the clicker. If she immediately stops whatever she is doing and looks at you, then you know she is ready to start being weaned off treats. If your kitty does not acknowledge the sound, then you know you need to spend extra time training with the click-treat combination.

TIPS FOR SUCCESSFUL CLICKER TRAINING:

- Try using a clicker with a wristband, as it will stay tethered to you and prevent you from accidentally dropping it.
- Place the treats in a baggie. You only have two hands, and a baggie allows you to keep the treats close at hand yet still hands-free.
- Keep all of your clicker training sessions short and sweet. Siamese cats learn better in bursts of one to three minutes instead of longer sessions.
- The clicker is not a remote control to cue your Siamese cat into doing something. The clicker only marks the moment your cat does something worth rewarding.
- Keep the clicker in a safe place, out of reach of mischievous children who may think it is a toy.

Do not be discouraged if it takes more time than you anticipated for your cat to respond to clicker training. A common mistake is to expect immediate results, but some cats take more time to respond to the clicker. Also, just because your Siamese cat has responded to the clicker for one type of behavior, do not assume it will automatically work for other behaviors.

CHAPTER 7
Potty Training Guide

> *As soon as the new owner takes the kitten home, I always recommend putting the kitten into the litter box and then allowing it to jump out on its own. Throughout the day, keep putting the kitten into the litter box repeatedly to familiarize the kitten with its litter area and the surrounding area. It is going to be exploring the first few days and will need reminders of where the toileting area is."*
>
> KAREN SPOHN
> *Candi Dasa cattery*

Whether you are a first-time cat owner or a veteran, potty training your new cat is a priority. Most kittens arrive at their new homes already knowing how to use a litter box, thanks to the helpful guidance of their mothers. Older adopted cats will generally just need a short refresher course on how to use the litter box.

Litter training is a simple affair, as cats instinctively want to bury any evidence after doing the deed. However, if your new Siamese cat needs some pointers, then the tips in this chapter will provide a goldmine of information.

Types of Cat Litter

Choosing the best type of litter for your cat is not as easy as grabbing a bag off the shelf at the pet store. There are a few types of cat litter available, but most of them fall into three different categories: clay-based, biodegradable, and silica-based. The best will depend entirely on your cat's preferences.

Litter boxes should be scooped daily, removing urine clumps and fecal matter. There should be at least three inches of litter in the box to provide ample depth for absorbing urine and let your cat dig a bathroom spot. A regularly cleaned litter box is essential for your cat's health.

> *Kittens are litter trained by the mom cat. So use the same type of litter and litter box the breeder or rescue has been using. Keep the litter box close to where the cat is being kept at first; then, after the cat has the freedom of your home, the litter box can be moved to a convenient place.*
>
> KATHLEEN RUSSELL HOOS
> *Blakewood Cattery*

Clay cat litter

Clay cat litter is the most affordable. Clay is used in litter because of its ability to quickly absorb moisture from the cat's urine. Plus, as an added bonus, clay litter provides natural odor control as it neutralizes urine.

However, as clay litter becomes soiled, its ability to absorb liquid and odor weakens. Traditional clay litter needs to be cleaned and changed regularly. Clay litter does not clump so that it can easily be removed with a scoop. Instead, the entire litter box needs to be emptied, cleaned, and the cat litter changed every week.

Some types of clay litter are made with bentonite, which causes the clay to clump. Clumping cat litters means individual clumps of soiled litter can be removed with a scoop, along with any feces in the box. As a result, the litter box does not need to be changed as frequently as non-clumping litter; you just need to replenish the soiled litter that was removed.

Silica cat litter

Silica cat litter is made from crystallized silica gel. The silica used in this type of cat litter is similar to the small pouches you find as a preservative for some foods, medications, and other foods or items. Silica gel is extremely absorbent and provides excellent odor control.

Silica cat litters are an excellent option for cat owners who prefer a non-clay litter, as they produce less dust. However, if your cat consumes a large quantity of this litter, it can cause some serious health problems.

Biodegradable cat litters

Biodegradable cat litters are a great option for cat owners who prefer an ecologically friendly product. Often, biodegradable cat litters are made from recycled cat litter or plant-derived materials, such as corn, wheat, pine, beet pulp, and soybeans. Since these products are biodegradable, they will not clutter garbage dumps. So, some products can even be used as mulch.

However, it is not recommended to dump the soiled litter near garden areas, fruit trees, and berry bushes, as it can introduce unwanted diseases to people.

The best cat litter for you and your cat depends on how much time you want to spend cleaning your cat's litter box and if you are concerned about litter dust and other factors. Plus, you will need to take into consideration your cat's preferences.

The best way to dispose of cat litter

If you ask any Siamese cat owner their least favorite chore related to their furry friend, it is cleaning out the litter box. It is smelly, and soiled litter is not the lightest thing in the world. On the other hand, litter is a necessity for any home with a happy cat. So, what is the best way of dealing with a dirty litter box?

Put it in the trash

One of the best ways to dispose of your cat's soiled litter is by disposing of it in the trash. Your cat's litter box needs to be scooped at least once a day. Use the litter scoop to shake excess litter off the urine clumps and any stool, then place it in a garbage bag. Once all of the litter boxes are scooped in your house, tie the bag in a knot and toss it in the outside trash can.

Never scoop cat litter directly in the trash and let it sit there. Litter can become smellier with time, plus bits of cat litter dust contaminated with the cat's fecal matter can spread into the air every time the trash can is opened.

If you live in a rural area, you may have access to a burn barrel for your trash. Clay litter does not burn and will simply settle to the bottom of the pile. Some biodegradable and silica litters may burn, but there is always a possibility of airborne toxins.

Some new cat biodegradable litter brands claim that their litters can be used as mulch or compost, but there are some concerns you should be aware of before dumping your soiled cat litter into the compost box.

Cat feces can carry bacteria like E. coli. Cats that are allowed to roam freely outside can also become infected with a protozoal parasite called Toxoplasma gondii and shed this parasite in their stool. Once the parasite is released into the environment, it can easily infect other animals and humans. If you plan on using your cat's biodegradable soiled litter as compost or mulch, use it only in the flower garden and never in your vegetable garden.

What about flushing?

No types of clay litter are flushable. The clay can cause serious damage to your plumbing.

Some biodegradable litters are designed to be flushed. However, manufacturers only recommend flushing urine clumps and disposing of fecal matter in the trash. This is because even though modern waste treatment plants can remove most parasites, often T. gondii and other intestinal parasites are not caught and destroyed, meaning they stay in our water supply.

Types of Litter Boxes

Kittens start using a litter box at about four weeks, so they are 100 percent fully trained by the time they get to a new owner. Eventually you can change to any kind of litter box and litter, but to start, it's best to stick with what the breeder does. If the kitten is used to a covered box and clumping litter, start there. If you want to change to something else, do it once the kitten is fully acclimated to its new home, then offer both; the kitty should get used to the new box.

KATHRYN BRADY
Katsmith

Not all litter boxes are created equal. Cats, Siamese cats especially, can be quite particular about their bathroom facilities. Shape, size, depth, and many other attributes, can affect how your cat feels about her litter box.

Here is a closer look at some of the different types of litter boxes:

Open litter boxes

Open litter boxes are quite simple; often they are often called litter pans, as they are large, uncovered pans that you fill with cat litter. There is nothing sophisticated about them, but they do the job. They are easy to clean and transport. But since the pan does not have any barriers, there is nothing to prevent your cat from flinging her litter around.

Covered litter boxes

Covered litter boxes are basically a litter pan with a lid on top. Most of them come with a simple lid with a swinging door, but some can be quite elaborate with magnetized doors and a fancy door shape. However, the box can be gnarly to clean as there is a lack of ventilation. Also, some cats are afraid of the swinging door and will avoid using the box.

Disposable litter boxes

Just as the name implies, a disposable litter box is meant to be disposed of. These boxes do not need to be cleaned, as you throw them away once used. This is a great option if you are traveling with your cat, as you can just throw away the entire pan instead of hauling a week's worth of dirty litter

around. However, this is an expensive option if it is used to replace a permanent litter box.

Self-cleaning litter boxes

This litter box style is sometimes called a sifting pan, as it has a grate at the bottom that sits in the box to help with cleaning. The crate can periodically be sifted by moving the grate from side to side, letting the litter fall through the cracks, leaving you with the dirty clumps on top of the grate to put in the trash. But a word of caution — these litter boxes are not easy to deep clean.

High-sided litter boxes

High-sided litter boxes are one of the most popular types of boxes as higher sides prevent litter from spilling over the edges. Most Siamese cats love to dig in their litter before finding the perfect spot to go to the bathroom; the higher sides prevent litter from being flung all over the floor. One disadvantage is this type of box is hard to clean up, and you have to bend over the box.

Designer litter boxes

Designer litter boxes are basically litter boxes in disguise within a bench, end table, or a planter made to match your home's decor. One advantage is you can plant your cat's litter box in the middle of the room, and nobody will be able to tell the difference. On the other hand, it is easy to forget to clean the box as you do not see it.

How big should your litter box be?

Think about this question in human terms. The litter box is your cat's bathroom. Do you like a bathroom that is cramped for space or a toilet placed next to a drafty and noisy washing machine? What if you had to navigate a high wall to access the toilet in the dark?

This is how your cat feels if she has the wrong litter box. You may need to change the location of her litter box or even the box itself. If your cat's litter box feels too uncomfortable or difficult to use, then she will simply find a different bathroom spot, and trust me — you will not be happy!

Sometimes finding the perfect litter box for your Siamese cat may take a little trial and error. A little creativity can go a long way. Here are some non-litter boxes that work great as a little box:

- Under-the-bed storage boxes - These plastic boxes are extra-large with low sides for easy access — the ideal solution for the cat who loves to dig in her litter box.
- Garden potting trays - Many of these have enough length and width and are great for cats with mobility issues as they have low sides.
- Storage bins - Deep, plastic storage bins can double as your cat's litter box.

Take into consideration your cat's personality when deciding whether to choose a closed or open litter box. For example: If your Siamese cat is on the shy side and prefers to hide, maybe she would do better with a closed box.

Kittens and seniors tend to do better with low-sided litter boxes as they allow for easier entry and exit. For cats with poor aim or who spray or fling their litter everywhere, a litter box with higher sides will be needed to help reduce the mess.

Whatever style you choose for your cat, it should be large enough for your cat to comfortably squat inside and move around. Your cat will need enough room to make figure eights inside of the box while she digs around for the perfect spot without having to step out of the box.

Litter Box Training Basics

> *Keep the litter box, bed, food, and toys all in the same area for the first week or two. Once your kitten has mastered the layout of its home, move your litter box to any area that you find appropriate.*
>
> CAROL GAGATCH
> *Carolina Blues Cattery*

Follow these steps to litter train your Siamese kitten:

- Show your kitty the litter box as soon as she arrives at your house. Place your cat next to the box and let her sniff and examine it on her own terms. Once you have shown your cat the box, do not move it, as she may become confused.
- Place your Siamese kitten inside of the litter box immediately after eating or waking up from a nap. If you notice that your feline friend is behaving like she needs to go to the bathroom, such as sniffing at the floor or crouching, quickly pick her up and place her inside of the litter box.
- Generously reward your kitty with a treat, praise, or a toy when you notice she has just used the litter box.
- Never punish your Siamese cat for having an accident. This will only cause your kitty additional stress and anxiety, making training more challenging.

CLEANING AND MAINTENANCE

Your cat's litter box will need daily upkeep, as it will help to eliminate that dreaded "cat smell" and will make for a happy and healthy cat.

- Scoop the box daily to remove any urine clumps or fecal matter. Replace soiled litter as needed. Often, when it begins to smell, it is time to change the litter in the box for new litter.
- Every time your change the litter in the box, be sure to disinfect the box with a mild soap or a solution of water with white vinegar. Never use bleach or commercial disinfectants that can be harmful to your cat.
- If your cat has had an accident on the sides of the box, be sure to cleanse the areas with an enzyme cleaner to eliminate the scent that may encourage your kitty to go in that spot again.

- Do not forget to wash your hands with warm soapy water every time you touch your cat's litter box.

LITTER TRAINING A SENIOR SIAMESE CAT

The majority of older Siamese cats will have had experience using a litter box by the time you adopt them. But there may be some challenges if they have spent some time in a shelter or if the cat was an outdoor cat. Even if this is the case, all cats have the basic instincts to learn to use a litter box at any age.

The biggest challenge will be getting the cat used to the litter box. If your adopted Siamese cat was an outdoor cat, try filling the litter box with outdoor soil to begin with. As your cat gets more used to the litter box, replace part of the soil with cat litter. Gradually, increase the cat litter as your cat becomes familiar with the new texture and surface.

If your adopted cat has been in a shelter for a long period of time, perhaps the conditions were not ideal. Your cat will just need a refresher course on how to use a litter box. Follow the instructions above. Within no time, your Siamese cat will be an expert at using her litter box.

Dealing with Accidents

> "*Put the kitten in the litter box 10–15 minutes after eating. Stimulate with a warm damp washcloth or paper towel. Do not deviate from this for about two weeks until the kitten starts seeking out the litter on its own. Dr. Elsey's 'Cat Attract' is a great starter for new kittens; only a layer on top of clay litter is necessary. NEVER use clumping litter with kittens. It turns into concrete, and kittens tend to eat litter at first.*"
>
> JULIE ZWEMKE
> *Zelines*

Kitty accidents can be a pain in the neck, but they can easily be prevented if you clean up quickly, efficiently, and correctly. The majority of potty accidents happen for one of the following reasons:

- Your kitten does not quite understand where her designated litter box spot is.

- Your cat cannot easily access her litter box. Your cat needs quick and easy access to her litter box twenty-four-seven.
- Your cat suffers from a medical condition, which will be discussed below.

If you do not thoroughly clean and deodorize where your cat had an accident, it will lead to more accidents in the same area. Simply wiping up the mess might satisfy your eyes and nose, but there is an enzymatic scent only your kitten can smell that will lure her back to the same spot later on.

Follow this three-step cleaning process to deter any future potty accidents:

1. **Protect your own paws:** Before cleaning up your cat's mess, make sure to wear gloves to protect yourself from potential urine and fecal pathogens, especially if your Siamese cat is not fully vaccinated yet.

2. **Remove the mess**: For any type of accident, pick up any solids with a paper towel or baggie and blot up (do not rub) any excess liquid. Once you have removed the bulk of the mess, follow up by using damp towels or rags to gently blot away the rest of the smaller residue.

3. **Use a good enzymatic neutralizer for pet accidents:** Avoid using any ammonia-based cleaning products as they may enhance the urine smell, which will make the spot irresistible for your cat. The best cleaning products will not mask the scent or simply clean up the accident, but they will neutralize the enzymes that entice your cat to pee or poop in that same spot. Look for products that are specifically designed for cleaning up after cats.

WHEN POTTY TRAINING RELAPSES

Nothing can be more disheartening than to discover your well-behaved Siamese cat regressing to bad bathroom manners. If your Siamese cat is suddenly relieving herself in a different place than her litter box, there's probably a good reason.

Medical problems – Bathroom accidents may be a sign of medical conditions, such as urinary tract infections or parasites. Your veterinarian will be able to rule out any possible medical issues.

Submissive/excitement urination – Some Siamese kittens may temporarily lose bladder control when they become overly excited. Often, this occurs during playtime. Involuntary urination or defecation is not a potty-training issue, as your cat simply has no control over it and is unaware that she just soiled herself.

Hormonal behavior - As your Siamese cat matures, she will undergo hormonal changes. Marking territory is a common behavioral trait for both male and female cats. If your cat is marking inside the house, then return to the first steps of potty training. If the problems persist, you can consider using a belly band designed to prevent her from marking.

A belly band for cats looks like a big Band-Aid or diaper that wraps around your Siamese cat's rear. Often, the belly band has a waterproof shell with an absorbent liner, which prevents any unwanted accidents in your house. Most styles are reusable and machine washable.

New environment – Just because your cat knows how to use her litter box in your house does not guarantee that she will know how to act when placed in a new setting. If you are traveling or visiting a friend's house, go back to the basic potty-training methods until you can trust your Siamese again.

Fear or anxiety – If your Siamese cat is afraid of loud noises such as fireworks or thunderstorms, she may lose control of her bladder and/or bowels. If this happens, try to isolate the sounds that frightened her and help her learn to associate good memories with those noises.

Common Problems

Why is my cat pooping outside of her box?

One of the main reasons your cat is pooping outside of her box is because it is too small.

Commercial litter boxes sold in pet stores are often designed for kittens and not full-grown adult Siamese cats. If your feline friend is having trouble finding the perfect spot in its small litter box by hanging her rear over the edge of the box to eliminate her waste, or if you find waste or urine or feces beside the box or outside of it, you most likely need a larger litter box.

If you need a bigger litter box, look for utility tubs, small kiddie playpools, or even a small sandbox. There is no need to be restricted to what is provided at your local pet store. Basically, if it is waterproof, you can put litter in it, and your cat can get in and out of it easily, then it will work as a litter box.

Another reason your feline friend may be urinating and pooping outside of her litter box could be a medical condition. If you suspect your cat is sick, call your vet immediately.

How can I stop my cat from tracking her litter and feces around the house?

There are a few reasons why your kitty is tracking litter and feces around the house. Some of these problems are easier to resolve than others:

- **Medical issues** – If your cat is in pain, it may be difficult for her to enter or exit the litter box, so she will avoid shaking her paws off before leaving the box. Arthritis, hip dysplasia, or other chronic issues make it uncomfortable for cats to jump in and out of their litter boxes. Litter boxes with sloped walk-up entrances or low-bottomed entryways are preferable for cats with mobility issues.
- **Dirty litter box** – A clean litter box eliminates poop from being tracked around the house. Siamese cats are notoriously fastidious about the cleanliness of their litter boxes. Be sure to keep your cat's litter box clean and scoop up any fecal matter and dispose of it as soon as possible.
- **Trim the fur on your cat's paws** – Some Siamese cats grow a lot of fur between their toes. If you keep your cat's fur on her feet trimmed, there will be less material for litter or feces to stick to.
- **Stool consistency** – Your cat's poop should be firm, formed, and consistent. If it is watery or soft, be sure to talk to your vet. Soft stools may be an indication of inflammatory bowel disease, parasites, food allergies, or other issues. Dietary changes, such as a change in cat food or stress, may cause loose stools. Any condition that causes loose stools to be softer than normal will contribute to poop being tracked around the house.

Troubleshooting

Consider purchasing a rug that is designed to catch litter particles. Place the rug or mat at the edge of your cat's litter box so she will walk on it when she exits the litter box. Some types of litter are designed to keep litter tracking to a bare minimum. Another option is to get a larger litter box.

Why doesn't my cat cover her poop?

Wild felines cover their excrement for two reasons — one is to keep their presence hidden from predators. The second reason is as a sign of submissiveness for more dominant felines. These more dominant cats almost never bury their feces, instead often leaving their excrement on a clump of grass, making it appear elevated and more prominent.

So, one logical reason why a domesticated cat refuses to bury her poop is because she is the dominant cat in the house. However, there are other factors why your cat is avoiding this natural cat behavior.

Declaring territory - Wild felines, such as tigers, jaguars, and leopards, do not bury their feces when competing for territory. Your domesticated cat may decide not to bury her poop to let other cats, or even you, know that she is declaring this spot as her own.

Personality - Some cats have a clean fetish and dislike getting their paws dirty. Often in this case, the cat will attempt to cover the fecal matter by swiping its paws on the floor or wall beside the litter box. Cats that choose not to cover their feces often are doing what comes naturally to them. Perhaps the mother cat never taught her kittens how to bury their feces, so they never really learned.

Litter box issues - When it comes to litter boxes, size does matter. Perhaps your cat's litter box is too small for her to turn around inside or bury her poop. Some cats are very finicky and do not like the feel of the litter under their paws. Or maybe the box is too dirty, and she would rather not spend any extra time there. If you suspect one of the above, try switching up your cat's litter to a new brand or upgrade to a larger litter box.

Medical issues - There are no specific medical issues that may cause your cat to stop burying her feces. But if you notice your cat is experiencing pain or discomfort, whether it's while going to the bathroom, in her paws, or just in general, that may deter her from spending more time in the litter box than necessary, or if you suspect your cat is sick or in pain, call your veterinarian immediately.

Why is my cat avoiding her litter box?

Cats naturally want to urinate and defecate in their litter box, but if they have a reason to avoid the litter box, they may urinate in the bathtub and defecate on your rugs. Litter box avoidance will occur at some point in your cat's life and occurs when the cat associates her litter box with a negative experience and may decide to take her business outside the box to the bathtub or your rugs.

Why the bathtub? Your bathtub looks like a large, clean litter box to your cat, so it is an obvious second choice for most cats.

Why your rugs? Rugs are popular targets for cats to defecate. Pinpointing the exact reason why is a mystery. Perhaps they are attracted to the fabric or the fact that the rugs are easy to paw at, like a litter box.

Sometimes urinating or defecating outside of the litter box is a one-time occurrence, but other times it can turn into an undesirable habit. Below are some reasons why your cat has changed her bathroom habits and how to correct them.

- **Dirty litter box** – Cats are like humans; they like to have a clean bathroom. One of the reasons a cat may go looking for a new bathroom spot is because she has a dirty litter box. Maybe the litter is old, smelly, clumpy, and full of dried fecal matter or the litter box itself needs a deep cleaning.
- **Closed-in litter box** – Strangely enough, some cats dislike feeling confined while going to the bathroom. Enclosed litter boxes can be a deterrent for a cat who needs to use the bathroom.
- **Type of litter** – Cats are quite sensitive to change and texture. If you recently changed the brand of litter, that probably is the reason your cat has started going to the bathroom in your bathtub or on your rug. Siamese cats have strong preferences and tend to dislike scented litter.
- **Fear or pain is associated with the litter box** – If your cat has arthritis, a urinary tract infection, cystitis, or any health issue that can cause pain, this may be the reason she started looking for an alternative bathroom. If the pain occurs in the litter box, a cat may associate the pain with the litter box; the same goes if a cat is scared or startled while in the litter box.
- **Not enough litter boxes** – Remember, each cat should have its own litter box. If there are two cats in the household, then there should be two boxes in the house. If there are not enough boxes in the house, the cat may resort to peeing elsewhere.

> *Bad litter box habits can be hard to correct. But it can be done! One of the best ways is to get a very large litter box with very high sides. Make sure litter is at least four inches deep. Cats love to dig and cover up their smells. Allowing them to dig will help correct issues. Always having an extra litter box around the house is a must. Giving your cat an option will make for a happy cat.*
>
> AMANDA WILLIAMS
> *AW Cattery*

The best way to ensure your Siamese cat happily uses her litter box is to identify the problem that is causing litter box avoidance. You may need to take your cat to the vet to rule out any medical problems. Be sure to regularly clean out your cat's litter box, change the placement of the box it a more private place in the house, or even switch to an unscented litter.

Toxoplasmosis

Toxoplasmosis is caused by a parasite called T. gondii.

It is very rare for humans to get toxoplasmosis from cats. Generally speaking, house cats that are not allowed to leave the house do not carry T. gondii. Wild cats or cats that are allowed to hunt outside are more likely to carry T. gondii. Cats do not normally show symptoms of toxoplasmosis, even if they are the host.

In North America, the most common way to be infected by the toxoplasmosis parasite is by eating uncooked meat or unwashed fruits and vegetables. Most people who are infected with toxoplasmosis have no symptoms. People who develop symptoms may experience one or more of the following:

- A fever
- A headache
- Muscle aches and pains
- Sore throat
- Swollen lymph nodes, especially around the neck

These symptoms can last for a few weeks and often resolve on their own without the need for medical treatment.

However, T. gondii can cause more serious symptoms for people with a weakened immune system, as they can develop the following:

- A lung infection, causing fever, shortness of breath, and cough
- Brain inflammation, causing headaches, confusion, coma, and seizures
- An eye infection, causing blurry vision and eye pain

IS IT SAFE TO BE AROUND MY CAT DURING MY PREGNANCY?

Yes, but you should take a few precautions. Toxoplasmosis can harm an unborn baby if the mother is infected during the pregnancy. It can cause a miscarriage, neurological defects, blindness, and other undesirable symptoms. Many of these symptoms may not be apparent at birth but become more evident as your child grows.

As mentioned above, cats pick up this parasite by consuming small rodents, birds, and so on. This is another reason to keep your cat indoors. Infected cats eliminate the parasite in their fecal matter. The T. gondii parasite needs one to two days after being passed to become infectious.

There are a few rare cases of a pregnant woman inadvertently ingesting contaminated cat feces by inhaling the litter dust while cleaning out the litter box. Here are some suggestions from the Centers for Disease Control (CDC) on how to prevent toxoplasmosis:

- Have someone who is healthy and not pregnant change your cat's litter box daily. If that is not possible, be sure to wear gloves and a disposable face mask. It is important to clean the litter box daily, as the parasite has an incubation period of one to two days. Dispose of the face mask after each cleaning. Wash hands with warm, soapy water afterward.
- Wash your hands with warm, soapy water after any exposure to sand, soil, raw meat, or unwashed fruits and vegetables.
- Avoid drinking untreated water from a well, particularly if visiting developing countries.
- Wash and peel all fruits before eating them.
- Wear gloves while gardening or handling sand from a sandbox. Wash your hands afterward.
- Do not eat raw meat, poultry, or fish.

Cats and Crate Training

Crate training is not as common with cats as it is with dogs, but it is worth the effort. Crates take the stress out of car rides, vet visits, traveling, or staying at a hotel or with friends.

Kittens generally embrace the crate more quickly than an older cat, but even the most set-in-her-ways feline can accept the crate. One of the most common reasons cat owners do not take their cat to the veterinarian as often as they should is because their cat hates the crate. Most felines only see the crate when it is time to go somewhere unpleasant, such as the groomer or the veterinarian. Your Siamese cat is smart and may quickly associate the crate with dreadful experiences.

Teach your kitty to associate the crate or travel carrier with positive, fun experiences. By training your Siamese cat to love the crate, you will be able to safely confine and transport your cat wherever necessary, rather than playing hide-and-seek when trying to place your terrified cat in the crate during an emergency. If your cat happily accepts the crate, it means she will be less stressed out and happier in her crate.

INTRODUCE THE CRATE

Start off by making the crate appear to be another piece of furniture. Place it on the floor in the corner of the room for your cat to explore at her own leisure. Place a soft, fluffy blanket that smells like your cat inside to make the crate seem more appealing, and toss a small handful of treats inside. Take the door off the crate so your kitten can come and go as she pleases. After that, it is only a matter of time until the scary and strange wear off.

PUT THE DOOR BACK ON

It may take two weeks or more for your cat to feel comfortable inside of the crate. Once that happens, put the door back on the crate and wait until your cat goes into the crate on her own accord. Then, softly close the door while using a calming voice. The goal of this is to teach your cat that there is nothing to be scared of and let her know it is perfectly normal for her to be inside the crate with the door shut.

After a minute or so, let your feline friend out and generously praise her and give her a treat. Play with her using one of her toys that is only reserved for special occasions. Your goal is to teach your cat that going into the crate is a positive experience and there is no need for upset feelings.

BUILD ON REPETITION

Repeat these sessions at least once a day for about two weeks, building up the time your cat is inside the crate longer and longer each time. Once your cat is able to stay in the crate with the door shut for ten minutes while remaining calm, then attempt to pick up the crate with your cat inside and walk around the house, and then let her out. Do not forget to praise her profusely. Repeat another day, but this time walk to the car and sit in the car with your cat while talking to her gently.

Soon, after two or three weeks, you should be able to take your Siamese cat for car rides without having her throw a fit. With time, your cat will learn that the crate, most of the time, is a positive experience, and going to the vet will not be the only association she has with the crate.

Here are helpful hints for persuading your cat to go inside of the crate:

- Spray some synthetic pheromones inside of the crate to help entice your kitty to go inside of the crate. Pheromones help cats and kittens feel calm, especially during stressful situations.
- If you have a hard-cover crate, throw in a ping-pong ball and create an instant kitty playground.
- If your Siamese cat is motivated by treats, be sure to leave some tasty snacks inside the crate for your kitty to discover. Soon your kitten will associate the crate with a magical treat-giving box.

Never give up on crate training, as it is the safest way to transport your cat. Never transport your cat without a crate or carrier, as it prevents her from distracting you while driving or being injured if you have to brake suddenly or are in an accident. Plus, a loose cat can easily escape from the car when you open the door.

If you adopted a Siamese cat who is terrified of the crate or carrier, do not expect her behavior to change overnight. A common mistake made by new cat parents is rushing through the process and expecting immediate results. Cats do not like to be rushed. Be sure to give your cat plenty of time. You need to pause on certain steps or even go backward for a week or two. Once your Siamese cat has mastered the step, then you can move on to the next.

Remember, your cat will associate the crate with the places you take her in it. If you only place your cat in the crate to go to the groomer or vet, it is likely she will start to dislike the crate again. Every few days, place your cat in the crate and walk around the house or go for a short drive, then return home. Do not forget to praise your cat or visit a friend who will welcome your cat into her house with treats.

Legendary British-American actress Elizabeth Taylor owned a plethora of animals during her life. Siamese cats were some of her favorites. She even gifted a Siamese kitten named Marcus to James Dean, her costar in the 1956 film Giant, two weeks before his fatal car crash. Taylor described her animals as some of her "sweetest and most cherished friends."

CHAPTER 8
Traveling

Before hitting the road with your feline friend, take the time to choose the safest and most comfortable option for your Siamese cat. Ask yourself how much time you will be spending with your cat on your vacation. If she will be spending the majority of time alone, then she will most likely be happier left at home than tagging along with you on your journey.

By planning ahead, you and your cat will have a safe, stress-free trip.

Preparing to Travel with Your Siamese

Siamese cats work hard to define their territories and can suffer psychologically and physically when removed from them. Also, cats have other ritualistic behaviors. They can predictably be found in the same spot each day, almost as though they are following a schedule. For this reason, taking your kitty out of her well-honed territory can be very stressful.

Not only will your cat suffer without feeling secure inside of her territory, but a stressed cat is prone to health issues during your travels and even after you have returned home.

Still, there are situations when your feline friend must hit the road with you. In such cases, you will need the basics, such as a sturdy travel carrier, a portable litter box, and plenty of food and water. But there is one item that many feline parents neglect to bring along — comfort. Comfort to a cat means familiarity. No matter what your kitty's comfort items are, be sure to bring two or three along on your travels.

When they rub their faces on a certain object, cats release pheromones that can alter their behavior and emotional state. Pheromones help to alleviate your cat's stress and provide familiarity while traveling. The best choices for your Siamese cat's comfort packing list are her most commonly used items. That might be your cat's bed, favorite blanket, and one or two toys to make the trip more enjoyable for all.

Whether you are planning to travel with your Siamese cat for necessity or pleasure, you will need to take some steps to prepare for your cat's needs along the way. Car travel and air travel, especially longer trips, require some forethought. Never assume you will be able to find everything you need for your feline friend during the journey.

Here is a checklist to make sure you have everything for traveling with your cat:

- **Food** – Be sure to pack enough cat food for the duration of the entire trip, as switching your kitty's food may cause her to have an upset tummy. If you are planning on traveling for a longer period of time, research ahead of time whether your Siamese's regular cat food will be available at your final destination.
- **Water** – Throw in a bottle or two of clean drinking water to keep your furry friend hydrated throughout the journey. Never allow your cat to drink water from an unfamiliar source such as a creek, puddle, or pond.
- **Food and water dishes** – Do not forget to bring your cat's food and water dishes along. Be sure to place them in an area where you can easily reach them throughout the trip. If you are tight on space, look for a set of pop-off food dishes.
- **Crate or carrier** – Depending on your method of travel, you might need either a hard-cover crate or a soft-cover carrier. Make sure to choose a comfortable traveling case, as it will most likely be used as your cat's personal bedroom when you reach the final destination. Place one of your cat's favorite blankets inside the carrier. How to choose an appropriate crate is discussed in the following pages.
- **Toys** – Be sure to bring along a few of your Siamese's favorite toys for the journey, as this will keep her distracted during long-haul trips and also help to relieve stress.
- **Blankets and kitty beds** – A nice fluffy blanket will keep your Siamese warm during the journey, plus the familiar scent will keep her calm.
- **Collar, leash, and ID tags** – Be sure to place your cat's collar and ID tags on her before leaving the house, and do not remove them until you return home. If your Siamese cat is an adventure-seeker, she may escape to explore her new surroundings, so you may also want to invest in a GPS pet tracker tag.
- **Cleaning supplies** – Traveling with cats can get messy. Be prepared by bringing along potty pads, baby wipes, paper towels, disposable garbage bags, and, of course, a pet-friendly stain remover.

- **Medications** – If your Siamese cat is taking any type of medicine or supplements, make sure you have enough for the duration of your trip.
- **Health and vaccination certificates** – Do not forget to bring along your Siamese cat's medical information when traveling in case of an emergency.

Traveling by Car

Whether you are taking your Siamese cat on a short trip or a long journey, you will want to ensure your feline friend is comfortable and safe.

Avoid the temptation to let your Siamese cat sit in the front seat or roam freely about the vehicle while it is in motion. If you have a car accident due to being distracted by your cat, you could be held accountable. Even worse, you or your kitty or other parties could be seriously injured.

DOs

- Secure your Siamese cat inside of a hard-cover crate that has been anchored to the vehicle by using a seat belt or other secure means or placed on the floor.
- Bring along plenty of clean drinking water to keep your kitty hydrated, especially during the summer months.
- If you have the air conditioner on or a window open, make sure it is not directly blowing on your Siamese cat. If the window is open, make sure your cat cannot stick her head out or accidentally jump out.
- If your kitty suffers from motion sickness, ask your vet to prescribe a mild medication and follow the vet's instructions for administering it.
- Make your Siamese cat feel at home inside of her crate by bringing along some familiar items such as her blanket, chew toys, etc.
- Bring along a human buddy. Whenever possible, share the driving and cat caretaking duties with a friend or family member. That way, you will be able to use the facilities or grab a quick bite to eat knowing someone you trust is keeping a watchful eye on your feline friend.
- Bring along a portable litter box and stop occasionally to let your cat relieve herself.

DON'Ts

- Never transport your Siamese cat in the back of an open pickup truck.

- Do not allow your cat to sit in the front seat and hang her head out of the vehicle while it is in motion. She could be injured by particles of debris or get sick from breathing cold air forced into her lungs.
- Never leave your Siamese cat alone inside of a hot car. It only takes a few minutes for your cat to become overheated. This may cause irreversible organ damage or even death.

Photo Courtesy of April Tinnin Sapphire Kittens Cattery

- Do not feed your Siamese cat at least two hours prior to traveling in order to prevent motion sickness.

A year-round hazard is leaving your Siamese cat unattended in your car. In addition to the dangers of heat and cold, anytime you leave a cat alone inside the car, you are offering an unspoken invitation to pet thieves.

Like us, cats can get bored, so if your car ride is several hours or even days, you will need to prepare for stops along the way. Always have a plan that considers your cat's needs, and talk to your veterinarian if you are not sure how to plan for a long road trip.

Choosing the Right Crate for Long-Distance Car Travel

Whether your Siamese loves long road trips or quivers at the very thought of getting into the car, you will want to make the journey as comfortable and pleasant for her as possible. Feline travel crates are designed to provide a safe, enclosed place for your cat to travel in comfort. These crates often come with extra security features, such as fasteners to keep the crate secure while traveling.

Here are the factors to consider when choosing a travel crate for your Siamese cat:

Size – The crate should be big enough for your Siamese cat to sit, stand, lie down, and turn around in but small enough to keep her secure. A general rule of thumb is that travel crates should be no more than six inches longer than your kitty. A bigger crate may give your feline friend more space to move about, but this also means she may involuntarily slide around inside of the crate while the vehicle is in motion.

Soft vs. hard-cover – A soft carrier may be more comfortable for your Siamese. However, for car travel, a hard crate provides your cat with more protection if you get into an accident. Another advantage of hard-cover crates is that they are easier to clean up if your kitty has an accident or gets carsick.

Harness – Due to new state laws, many car crates come with a built-in harness, which allows a crate to be securely fastened to the seat belt for extra stability. By fastening the crate to the seat belt, you are creating a more secure ride for your Siamese cat, as the crate will not slide around on sharp corners or fly forward if you come to a sudden stop.

Visibility – Siamese cats are very curious by nature and love to observe their surroundings. Choose a crate that will give your cat an unhindered view and lots of fresh air. If your cat is nervous about car travel, then the more visibility, the better.

Traveling by Plane

> *When flying, you will have to go through security. If the kitty is nervous, you can ask for a private screening. Put a harness with a leash on the kitty. Then you will have a 'handle' to hold on to if something spooks the kitty, and the leash will prevent it from getting away from you just in case. Make sure the carrier fits under the seat, and bring everything you might need in case the kitty has an accident.*
>
> KATHRYN BRADY
> *Katsmith*

You might feel a little apprehension when you are planning on traveling with your cat on a plane. How can you keep your feline friend safe? Will she feel scared? Should you take her in the cabin with you? There are a lot of things to consider when flying somewhere with your Siamese cat. As long as you plan ahead, pack all of the necessary supplies like bowl, food, and litter, and meet all of the airline's requirements, your kitty and you will be just fine.

Generally, veterinarians and breeders do not recommend flying with your pet unless absolutely necessary. Ideally, a cat should not fly unless its owner is permanently moving to a new location or taking a long trip of two to three weeks minimum. This is because flying can be extremely stressful for your Siamese cat.

Air travel removes your Siamese cat from her comfortable home and familiar surroundings, forcing her into a strange environment with loud noises, bright lights, changes in air pressures and cabin temperature, and, to make matters worse, few opportunities to use the bathroom.

CARGO OR CARRY-ON?

When flying with your Siamese cat, you have two options — bring your cat into the cabin or check your cat to travel in the plane's cargo area. Your furry friend will typically be happier and safer if she can fly in the cabin with you. However, each airline has different rules and regulations as to where your feline friend will be allowed to spend her time during the flight, depending on her size.

Typically, your cat will be allowed to fly in the cabin as a carry-on if she is small enough to fit in a carrier under the seat in front of you. Most airlines have a weight limit of twelve to fifteen pounds for pets flying in the cabin, though there are some exceptions. Any larger than that, and your cat will usually have to travel in the cargo hold, along with the luggage and freight.

Each airline has its own policies regarding cats and travel. Check with the airline about any fees, restrictions, or unique requirements. Some airlines only allow a limited number of in-cabin pets per flight, so make sure there is still room before booking. You will also want to ask for pre-boarding since boarding early can make things easier when flying with your cat.

Every year, hundreds of thousands of pets fly in the cargo without incident, but there are many unknown variables that you have no control over once you hand your Siamese cat over to airline personnel.

Airlines do their best to make your cat comfortable in the cargo hold. However, baggage handlers are often just trying to get the plane loaded or unloaded on time. They are not paid to give your cat extra attention inside of her crate. Unfortunately, many pet owners have horror stories of their pets being injured, becoming seriously ill, getting lost, or even dying after flying in the cargo hold.

HOW MUCH DOES IT COST?

Prices vary from airline to airline, but the average price for your Siamese cat to travel in the cargo hold is approximately $75 each way. The average price for your cat to fly in the cabin with you can vary from $150 and up. The majority of airlines provide an online calculator so you can estimate the cost.

RESEARCH

Airline regulations are constantly changing, especially if you are traveling internationally. It is important to read through these rules thoroughly before traveling so your Siamese cat is not turned away before boarding the plane. To avoid this, a few days before flying, phone the airline company to double-check that you have all the required documents for traveling with your Siamese cat.

Some airlines require that cats be at least sixteen weeks old. Other airlines require your pet to have had her rabies vaccination more than thirty

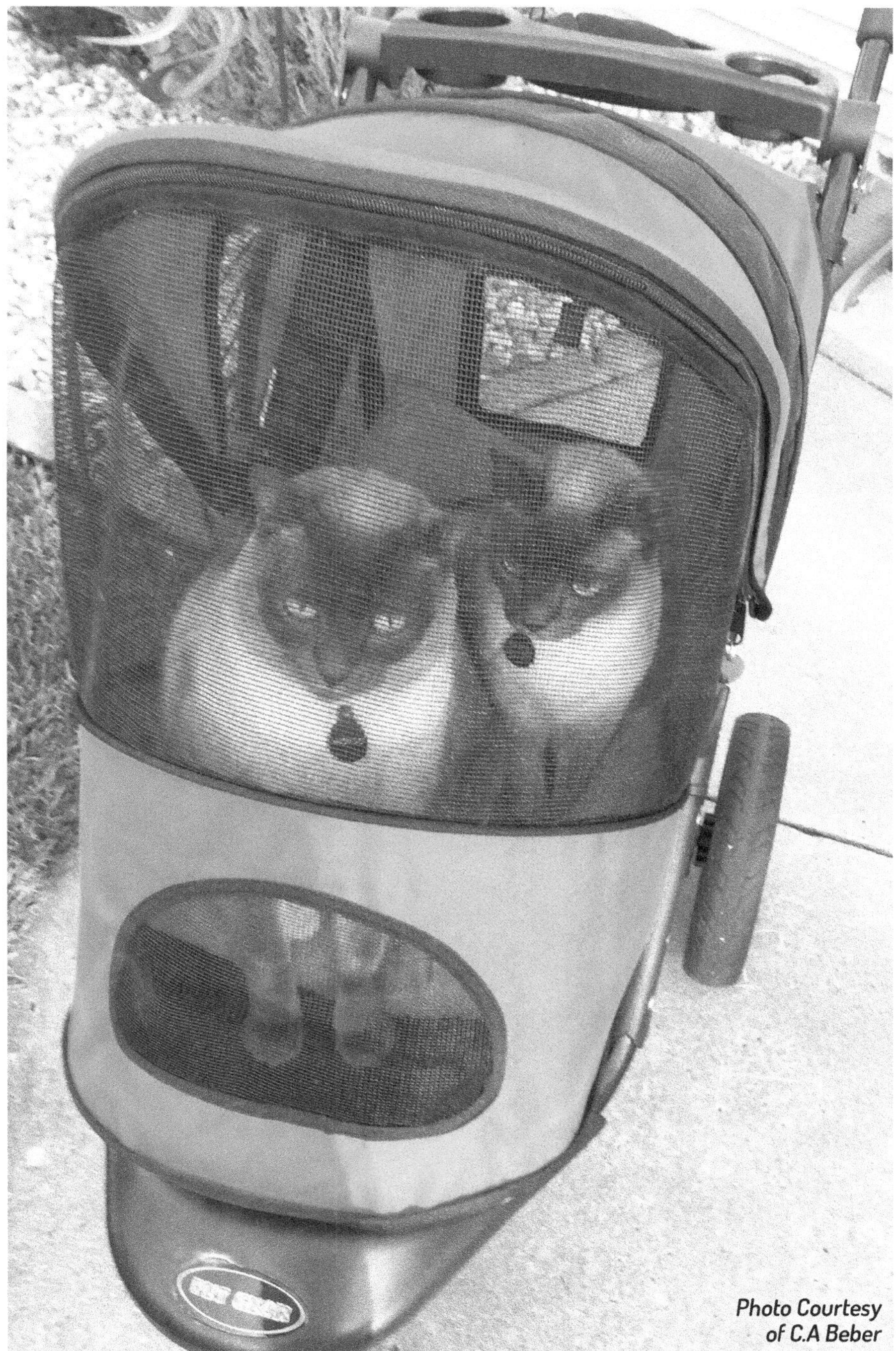

Photo Courtesy of C.A Beber

days prior to the flight. Unfortunately, many airlines do not allow pets on flights to Hawaii or certain international flights unless they are certified service pets.

Look for nonstop flights with no transfers. Avoid traveling with your Siamese cat during the holiday season when airports are busy, and flights are packed. This is to minimize the risks of any unexpected changes or cancellations.

Consider the weather in your final destination. If you are traveling somewhere cooler, choose flights in the middle of the day when the temperature is not as cold. If you are traveling somewhere warmer, choose flights later in the evening or early mornings before the temperature rises. Keep in mind, most airlines will not let your pet travel in the cargo hold if the temperatures are too extreme at the final destination.

The majority of airlines allow only a certain number of pets each flight, so always call the airline and make sure they have space for both you and your Siamese cat. Always make reservations for you and your cat at the same time to avoid unwanted last-minute surprises at the airport.

CONSIDER YOUR DESTINATION

If you are planning on traveling internationally or even to some U.S. states such as Hawaii or Puerto Rico, be sure to check local animal transportation regulations before purchasing your ticket. Many international destinations have a complicated process and/or lengthy quarantine periods, which may mean you will be separated from your Siamese cat for part or most of your trip.

Before traveling, research the departing and destination airport so that you know exactly where any pet-relief areas are located inside the airport. If you have flight transfers, your Siamese cat will thank you for letting her relieve herself and stretch her legs. If not, look for a private bathroom with a door that completely shuts and set up your cat's portable litter box inside of the bathroom.

CONSULT WITH YOUR VET

Before planning any flights with your Siamese cat, be sure to consult with your veterinarian about food, water, and medication. The American Veterinary Medical Association does not recommend sedating cats prior to flying. There are health risks with sedating cats, and certain airlines prohibit sedating pets without a certified note from a veterinarian.

If your Siamese cat is slightly overweight, your vet can formulate a weight loss plan to help the feline lose those extra pounds before the big journey. This is important, as obese cats are at a higher risk of having their airways collapse while traveling.

Many airlines require that your Siamese cat have a clean bill of health before flying. Your veterinarian can issue a health certificate stating that your kitty is healthy enough to fly and is up to date on her vaccinations. If the duration of your trip is longer than the certificate's validity, then you will need to get another certificate from a veterinarian while on vacation in order to meet the requirements of your Siamese cat's return flight.

AT THE AIRPORT

Make sure to arrive at the airport with plenty of extra time to avoid being stressed.

If your Siamese cat is traveling in the cargo hold:

Most airlines require you to arrive at least three hours before domestic flights and at least five hours before international flights. You may have to take your Siamese cat to a separate cargo drop-off section in the terminal, so review departure and arrival airport maps ahead of time to avoid confusion.

Be sure to paste a current picture of your cat on the crate along with her name. Also, you can tape a bag of food to the outside of the crate in case of a long delay. Be sure to have a current picture of your Siamese cat on your phone and a picture of her crate in case the airline accidentally misplaces your cat, which is not likely to happen, but it is better to be prepared than sorry.

If your cat is traveling in the cabin

Go directly to the passenger check-in desk, where the agent will request to see your cat's health certification and proof of immunizations.

Once you pay the pet carry-on fee, head directly to security. Deal with your personal items, such as computers, jackets, shoes, etc., before tending to your cat. Remove your Siamese cat from her carrier case and carry her through security while her carrier goes through the X-ray machine. To speed things up, do not forget to remove your cat's harness or collar so it does not set off the metal detector.

On the plane

Once you and your Siamese cat are on the plane, she cannot leave her carrier for the entire duration of the flight unless your cat has special certification such as an emotional support cat, etc.

Keep your Siamese well hydrated throughout the flight by using an attachable water dispenser. Your cat's ears can pop due to the pressurization upon take-off and landing. To avoid this, give your Siamese cat a few pieces of chewy jerky to munch on during this portion of the flight, but be careful not to give her too much, as she could get airsick.

In the cargo hold

Make sure you invest in a good quality hard-cover crate with adequate ventilation, waterproof bottom, spring-locked door, and no handles. Your Siamese cat should be able to completely turn around and also stand up in the crate without hunching over. Do not compromise on your feline's comfort make sure she has enough room to stretch out.

Go the extra mile to cable tie the crate's doors shut. Spring locks are hard to get open, but go the extra step to ensure no accidents happen.

Attach a latch water bottle with an easy-to-use water dispenser inside of the crate. Do not place it on the outside, as it could easily get knocked off as the baggage handlers transport your cat. Fill and freeze the water bottle the night before for dripless, refreshing hydration.

If your cat is hesitant to drink from the water bottle, entice her by filling the bottle with lukewarm chicken broth. Water dispensers have a ball inside of the cap that rolls around when touched, releasing water. You might have to encourage your Siamese cat by rolling the ball around and releasing the irresistible scent of chicken broth. Reward her when she drinks from the bottle and slowly wean her off the chicken broth by replacing it with water.

Place visible identification and documentation on your cat's crate. Make sure the following information is attached to the crate: your full name, flight information, name of your pet, picture of your pet, your home and cell phone number, any medical considerations, cat temperament issues (if any), and veterinary information.

Make sure your cat has her collar on with her ID tag. Inside of the crate, make sure your Siamese cat is comfortable with a soft blanket. Place some super-absorbent potty pads under the blanket just in case your kitty has an accident or two.

Upon arrival

If your Siamese cat traveled in the cargo hold, pick up your checked luggage upon arrival and go straight to your airline's specified location for cargo. Airlines often state that pets will be available for pick-up thirty minutes after the flight's arrival. If your cat is not picked up within four hours of arrival, the airline will hand the cat over to a veterinarian or boarding facility at your expense.

Whether your Siamese cat flew in the cabin or the cargo hold, take her to a private place, such as a bathroom, so she can stretch her legs and use her portable litter box. Even though the journey may seem complicated, you both will breathe a sigh of relief when you arrive at your final destination together.

Lodging Away from Home

If you plan on road-tripping with your Siamese cat, chances are you will be staying at a hotel, with friends or family, or in another type of rental at some point along your journey. If not planned properly, overnight stays in a new environment can cause you and your cat stress. If your vacation or trip away from home is not complete without your Siamese cat by your side, you'll be happy to know there are many cat-friendly options to bring your kitty along.

Hotel stays

Many hotel chains are not only cat-friendly nowadays but also give their feline guests the royal treatment. A recent survey by the American Hotel & Lodging Association discovered that almost 80 percent of luxury, mid-scale, and economy hotels in the United States now allow pets.

Researching cat-friendly hotels

Not all pet-friendly hotels welcome cats. Below are some tips to ensure your Siamese cat will be welcome at a hotel.

Talk directly with the hotel – Book directly with the hotel over the phone. This way, you will be able to ask any specific questions regarding the hotel's policies and fees for overnight pet guests. Ask the following questions:

- If there is a pet fee, is the fee per night or a flat rate for the entire stay?
- Does the hotel require a damage deposit?
- Is the entire hotel pet-friendly or only a designated floor? If the latter, ask whether the restaurants or lobby area are pet-friendly.

- Can you leave your cat in the hotel room alone, or does she need to be supervised? If so, how long does the hotel's policy allow your cat to be left unattended?
- Does the hotel offer cat sitters? If so, what are the costs and availability for your stay?
- Are there any charges associated with damages from your pet?

The majority of hotels charge a nominal fee for cats. The standard price per night is $25 to $50. Many major hotel chains or boutique hotels offer discounts for pets during the off-season.

Tips for a stress-free hotel stay

Before making your reservation, check the hotel's online website for photos of the room. Avoid hotel rooms that have carpet or leather furniture. Play it safe, and bring along extra blankets to throw over anything your feline friend may be tempted to scratch. As you may recall, Siamese cats scratch to help relieve stress and claim a new environment as their own.

If you are concerned about your Siamese cat "marking her territory," it might be worthwhile to bring some cat-specific stain and odor remover.

If you must leave your furry friend alone in a hotel room, even if it is for a short period of time, these steps will help you and your kitty avoid any problems:

- Do not leave your Siamese cat alone until she has become acclimated to the new space. Take the time to establish in your cat's mind that this room is her "new home."
- Try doing a few practices by leaving the room for a few minutes, then coming back inside. This will help your cat understand that if you leave, you will be returning promptly.
- Keep your time away as short as possible.
- If available, upgrade your room to a suite. By having two separate living spaces, you can place your cat's carrier in the furthermost corner from the hallway. This will act as a buffer, giving your kitty some space from those strange noises outside of her door.
- Tired cats are less likely to meow. Be sure to play with your Siamese cat before heading out.
- Pack something extra special to keep your cat distracted while you are out and about, such as a toy stuffed with a delicious treat. If your cat's mouth is busy, she will be less likely to scratch or meow.

- Help your Siamese cat relax by playing soft piano music, and leave it playing when you go out to cover any hallway noises.
- Use a calming diffuser with pheromones to help your cat relax.

Have a backup plan if you cannot leave your Siamese cat alone – If the hotel policy is that you cannot leave your furry friend alone in the room, make sure you have a backup plan. Many hotels offer additional services, such as a cat sitter for hire. Another option is to take your Siamese cat to a day spa or groomer for the day.

If the hotel lets you leave your kitty alone in the hotel room, always give the front desk staff a heads up and leave them your cell phone number in case of any noise complaints or other issues. Also, do not forget to place a DO NOT DISTURB sign on the door to prevent your cat from unexpectedly surprising the housekeeper.

Staying with friends and family

Today's society has become quite tolerant of cats, but not everyone wants a cat at their next family gathering. You are taking your Siamese cat into someone else's house. Ask where your cat will be allowed to go and what areas are off-limits. Also, if your cat accidentally goes to the bathroom on the carpet, clean up after her promptly.

If things do not work out as planned, have a contingency plan, such as a pet-friendly hotel nearby or a reputable boarding kennel. No matter how things go, send a thank-you card to express your gratitude and, if necessary, to apologize.

No matter where you are planning on staying, these are some helpful suggestions on how to minimize friction:

Ask first – Never just show up to stay at someone's house with your Siamese cat in tow. Always ask permission to bring along your furry friend. Not everyone wants a cat as a

It's no secret that Siamese cats hate being away from their humans, so if you're an avid camper, you may be wondering how to include your feline friend in this endeavor. Pets are allowed in all US national forests, but they are required to be leashed, so be sure to bring a harness along. Some campgrounds also charge extra for bringing a pet. Packing a litter box may seem like a nuisance, but whether or not you bring the box, you'll need to clean up after your cat's bathroom breaks. Cat feces can contain a parasite harmful to mammals and should not be left behind in the wilderness.

house guest. Even cat lovers appreciate an advance warning, as it allows them to kitty-proof their home, such as putting away those collectible porcelain figurines on display.

The strain of an unwelcome cat can permanently damage relationships. So, even if your Siamese cat was welcome somewhere in the past, never assume she is welcome again — ask first!

Talk it over - Another factor to take into consideration is if the host or other house guests may be allergic to cats, or maybe there are small children present who are uncomfortable around felines. Even well-meaning relatives or friends can inadvertently let your cat escape. That can be bad at home, but in a strange place, it can be a tragedy. So, make sure you discuss any concerns in advance with your host.

Be considerate - If your Siamese cat is prone to bad behavior, such as destructive chewing, nonstop meowing, scratching, or house-soiling, it is unfair to expect your host to welcome your cat into their house.

Boarding Kennels vs. Cat Sitters

You and your Siamese cat do everything together — from cleaning the house together to sitting in front of the fire on a cold winter day. You are two peas in a pod, which is why the very idea of leaving your best friend behind is so painful.

Unfortunately, there will be occasions when you cannot take your Siamese cat with you, meaning you will have to choose between boarding your cat in a kennel or hiring a cat sitter to watch her while you are out of town.

Who will care for your cat? Will her caregiver give her plenty of cuddles and ear scratches? Is your cat better off at home with a professional cat sitter, at a friend's house, or boarded at a local kennel? There is no ideal solution, but taking into consideration your Siamese's age, temperament, and needs will make the decision a little less worrisome.

Boarding Kennels

The best way to describe a boarding kennel is as a pet hotel for your Siamese.

Boarding kennels pride themselves on providing your cat with a safe environment. But just to be on the safe side, be sure to do your research beforehand to determine which kennel is right for your fur baby. Here are some things to consider:

How much space will your Siamese cat have?

Where will your cat stay? How big are the sleeping and play areas? – Will she have enough space to stretch out, exercise, and play? Will she have a scratching post, or can you bring your cat's post? Siamese cats are high-energy felines and do not do well locked in a small, cramped, enclosed space.

How many caregivers will be around during the day and at night?

You are paying for the kennel to care for all of your cat's needs, so it is important your cat receives the proper amount of attention. Ask how many people work at the kennel throughout the day and how they interact with the cats. Also, check into their experience and certification.

What are the fees, requirements, and inclusions?

Check out the kennel's fees and understand exactly what is included in the price per night. For example: Does the fee cover food and additional services, or do you have to provide the food and pay extra for grooming? Depending on the kennel's regulations, you might have to take your cat to a health screening to make sure she is up to date on her vaccinations before a kennel will accept her.

What is the kennel's reputation?

Look at the kennel website and social media pages for customer reviews or testimonials. If you know any friends who have boarded their pets at a certain kennel before, ask them for an honest opinion.

Your Siamese's stay at the boarding kennel includes grooming, attention, and daily exercise. Depending on the kennel you choose, a variety of packages and prices will be offered that cater to your kitty's individual requirements. If you are considering this option, here are a few advantages and disadvantages:

Advantages of boarding kennels

- Boarding kennels provide a secure environment with experienced, cat-loving employees who will constantly monitor your Siamese cat to prevent any incidents.
- Your cat will follow a strict schedule during her stay, which will reduce her stress levels. From your Siamese cat's first day there, she will be fed and exercised according to a schedule.

- Often there is a veterinarian on-site or on-call if there are any emergencies. This option is especially helpful if your Siamese cat has chronic health problems, as she will receive constant monitoring.

Disadvantages to boarding kennels

- With all the different pets staying at the kennel, things can get quite chaotic and noisy at times, which can be stressful for all cats. If your Siamese cat tends to get nervous in a new environment or around other cats or dogs, maybe boarding your cat might not be the best option.
- Although the kennel staff will do their best to keep everything in check, certain situations can get out of control. There is a small risk factor if your Siamese cat accidentally gets into a scuffle with another pet.
- Depending on the size of the boarding facility, staff could mix up food, toys, or blankets between different cats. Often, this does not cause too many problems, except perhaps an upset tummy.
- Keep in mind, if you leave your Siamese cat at a boarding kennel, she will spend the majority of her time alone inside of her kennel without any personalized stimulation.

Boarding kennels have the right to refuse admittance to any cat if the pet owner lacks adequate proof of a cat's vaccinations or if the cat has serious health conditions or displays aggressive behavior.

Keep in mind — Siamese cats do not handle stress very well and may develop health issues while in the kennel or after they return home.

Cat Sitters

A cat sitter is someone who cares for your cat in your home while you are temporarily absent. Typically, the cat sitter will stay in your house or drop by several times a day while you are away, allowing your Siamese cat to feel safe and secure in her own territory. Having a cat sitter stay overnight is the ideal solution if you prefer not to leave your feline alone at night.

Advantages to a cat sitter

- While you are away, your Siamese cat is in the comfort of her own home. There is no need to worry about your feline friend being exposed to a new environment, people, or other animals.
- The risk of accidents or injury is reduced because a single person is devoted to caring for your Siamese cat.

- Your cat sitter will carefully follow all of your care instructions for your cat and may even water your plants if you ask. If you have a younger kitty, you can teach the cat sitter how to reinforce your kitty's training.
- A cat sitter will directly communicate with you if there are any problems, etc. The direct line of communication will give you peace of mind, so you can focus on your travels.

Photo Courtesy of Carmen Medina

Disadvantages to a cat sitter

- A cat sitter needs to come into your house, and it is imperative you and your Siamese cat trust her or him. If your cat is protective of her home or does not react well to new people, perhaps a cat sitter is not the best option.
- Having a cat sitter stay in your home requires extra preparation, such as readying the guest bedroom.
- During the holiday season, it can be almost impossible to find a reliable cat sitter. Be sure to book ahead of time.
- If you hired a cat sitter to drop by a few times a day, and there's bad weather, the person might not be able to get to your house regularly.

Choosing the right sitter – Try to choose someone whose energy level and personality match that of your cat. For example, leaving your playful kitty with an elderly relative is a recipe for disaster. Make sure you feel comfortable with the cat sitter and that he or she understands your Siamese's individual needs.

Finding a professional and responsible cat sitter should not be taken lightly; after all, the cat sitter will be responsible for your cat's welfare, and you are entrusting him or her with the keys to your house. Here are a few suggestions to help you find a reputable cat sitter for your feline:

- **Ask your veterinarian** – If your Siamese cat is elderly or has health issues, finding a cat sitter with a good recommendation from your vet will give you peace of mind, especially if there is a medical emergency.
- **Word of mouth** – Anyone can look good on paper, but a qualified, reputable cat sitter will come recommended by a close friend or a relative.
- **Ask for references** – Any reputable cat sitter will be able to provide you with a list of regular clients who would be more than willing to verify the person's professionalism.
- **Look for a certified cat sitter** – There are two nation wide agencies that train and certify cat sitters: Pet Sitters International (PSI) and the National Association of Professional Pet Sitters (NAPPS). Be sure to check out their web pages to locate a certified cat sitter in your locality, plus you can check out reviews from previous clients.

Location – Ideally, you want someone who can stay at your house to maintain your Siamese cat's regular routine and schedule. This involves keeping your cat on the same feeding and sleeping routine as when you are at home. If you must change your cat's routine, get her used to the changes a few weeks ahead of time to prevent separation anxiety or other issues.

If you plan on leaving your cat at a friend's house while you are away, you might want to get her familiar with the new location a few times before actually leaving your cat there for an extended stay.

Details – Just as parents leave a checklist for a babysitter, you can make a checklist for your cat sitter. Include important information such as the vet's phone number and address, any medications your cat needs to take while you are away, allergies, feeding schedule, the closest twenty-four-hour emergency veterinary clinic, and any behavioral problems.

Share with the cat sitter any house rules for your Siamese cat, such as whether she is allowed on the furniture and how often she gets a treat — basically, any information you feel will keep your feline feeling happy, and secure while you are away.

Do not drag out goodbyes – Your Siamese cat is used to seeing you leave the house without her, so do not make a big production of your departure this time. If you do, you might make your kitten anxious. Be confident and casual when you say goodbye; both of you will be more relaxed.

Keep watch – If you are still uncomfortable about leaving your fur baby with a stranger, you could invest in a pet camera. Many smart pet cameras are designed to let you interact with your pet.

Relax – Now, take a deep breath and relax! You have taken all of the necessary steps to ensure that your Siamese cat has a pleasant experience while you are away, so enjoy your trip.

Carefully consider the advantages and disadvantages of each cat-care option. If you cannot decide which is the best choice for your feline friend, you can always try a short stay at a boarding kennel and another with a cat sitter before your actual planned trip to see how your cat reacts.

CHAPTER 9
Nutrition

A balanced and nutritious diet is essential to keep your Siamese cat healthy, but providing her with the right amount of nourishment can be tricky.

Obesity is one of the most common cat problems observed by veterinarians and often is due to an unbalanced diet of too many treats and not enough wholesome ingredients. In this chapter, you will learn everything you need to know about feeding your feline friend at every stage of her life.

Importance of a Wholesome Diet

"

I always chose a blend of a dry raw diet mixed with regular kibble. I use Instinct Raw Boost mixed with Royal Canin for Siamese. Royal Canin for Siamese is a wonderful food choice, especially for cats who binge eat, as it is a circular kibble requiring the cat to thoroughly chew it, thus preventing cats from swallowing their food whole and throwing it up later. Consider the addition of probiotics to the cat's diet. There are several brands out there that are easy to add to food or drinking water.

KAREN SPOHN
Candi Dasa cattery

"

Every Siamese cat is different. Some Siamese love to eat, while others are picky eaters or have a sensitive stomach, and there are also cats with dietary sensitivities. Deciding on what to feed your cat is a very personal choice; however, her diet will have a direct impact on her health and happiness.

Just like humans, cats require essential nutrients to develop properly and stay healthy. The wrong diet can lead to a life of health issues and obesity; on the other hand, the right diet can keep your cat slim, healthy, and in tip-top shape.

The old saying "you are what you eat" applies to your Siamese cat as much as yourself. Cat food made with high-quality ingredients equals a better quality of life, resulting in fewer infections, digestive issues, skin conditions, and so on. The impact of a wholesome diet does not end there, as it can also directly impact your cat's personality and behavior.

Cats must get vitamins and minerals from their diet. Cats have a higher requirement than dogs for dietary protein, which is made up of amino acids.

Your cat's behavior is a direct result of activity in her central nervous center. If she is not receiving the necessary nutrients, she will be lethargic, moody, and inactive. Here are a few examples of how the food you give and the frequency with which you feed your Siamese cat will impact her mood and behavior.

Unbalanced diet – Many health and behavioral issues in cats are caused by a poorly balanced diet. For example, a diet deficient in nutrients may cause your Siamese to suffer from frequent urinary tract infections that cause her to become irritable due to discomfort and pain. Make sure your Siamese only eats well-balanced, high-quality cat food to maintain good mental and physical health.

Inadequate food – If your Siamese cat is not consuming enough calories throughout the day, she will be hungry and may engage in disruptive behaviors such as scavenging through your garbage or eating feces. Cats who are not receiving sufficient nutrients in their diet may develop a condition called pica, which causes them to eat non-food items such as soil and plants.

Pet food ingredients – The ingredients in your kitten's pet food may also affect her behavior. For instance, research has found that senior cats who receive a diet rich in antioxidants are able to learn complicated tasks faster than cats who do not. Studies have shown that senior cats who have always received a high-quality cat food suffer from fewer behavioral changes common to cognitive decline.

A well-balanced diet will promote stable blood sugar levels throughout the day, which will directly affect your Siamese cat's serotonin levels. Serotonin not only improves your cat's mood but also her concentration and behavior. Another advantage of a wholesome diet is your Siamese cat's immune system will be in excellent condition.

Talk to your veterinarian before changing your Siamese cat's diet. Your vet will recommend a brand of food that is suitable for your cat's age, size, weight, medical history, and lifestyle.

Here are some common health issues related to your Siamese cat's diet:

- **Heart disease** – Cats often have issues with heart disease, especially if their diet is not well-balanced. Increased levels of sodium are one of the main factors of heart disease. Since high-quality commercial foods are low in sodium, the main source of sodium is probably coming from those table scraps you are slipping your kitty under the table.
- **Diabetes** – Overweight cats tend to develop diabetes as they age. There is no known cure for diabetes. A cat with diabetes will require daily insulin shots, a special diet, and extra medical attention. The best and only prevention is to keep your Siamese cat on a healthy diet and give her an active lifestyle. Avoid cat food that contains starchy fillers and sugar, which offer little to no nutritional value and will spike your cat's blood sugar level.

- **Obesity** – Obese cats are prone to arthritis, diabetes, breathing issues, high blood pressure, and cancer. Decreased life expectancy is linked to obesity in cats. Your Siamese cat does not need excessive calories each day. Be sure to follow the instructions on the container for her weight, size, and age.
- **Pancreatitis** – Pancreatitis is caused by a diet high in fats. Consult with your vet to see if your cat's current dietary fat intake may be increasing her risk of pancreatitis.

What about making your own cat food at home? Experts highly recommend avoiding this route unless you have the help of a veterinary

Photo Courtesy of Tom Jimmerson

nutritionist to help you. Siamese cats are only eight to ten pounds, and changing one ingredient in their diet can change impact their entire diet.

What about a vegetarian diet for your Siamese cat? A vegetarian or vegan diet may be a healthy choice for you and your family, but it is not a good idea for your cat. Unlike humans, cats require a specific number of vitamins, minerals, and proteins that only come from meat.

What about a raw meat diet? Even though raw meat is an essential part of a wild cat's daily diet, it is unnatural for a house cat. In the wild, a cat will eat the entire animal or bird it catches, not just the meat. Meat alone would be deficient in vitamins, minerals, and amino acids. Plus, bacteria in raw meat, such as salmonella and E. coli, can make both you and your cat very sick.

FOOD ALLERGIES AND SENSITIVITIES

Food allergies and sensitivities are not the same thing. It is important to take into consideration how a particular food affects your Siamese cat. If your cat's energy level is normal for her age, if her coat and skin are healthy, if her stools are brown and well-formed, and if she appears to be healthy, then her food is doing its job.

However, if your Siamese cat has diarrhea, skin issues, or an extremely itchy coat, your feline friend may have a food sensitivity. In this case, discuss the issue with your veterinarian. He will be able to help you create a feeding plan that works best for your kitty's health. Often, your veterinarian will place your cat on an elimination diet and slowly reintroduce foods to determine what foods are causing the allergic reaction.

Food allergies are often referred to as "adverse reactions to food," in which the immune system is involved. Food allergies present an immediate immunological response, such as anaphylactic shock, which may mean your cat is having difficulty breathing. In this case, you should take your feline friend to the nearest veterinarian clinic immediately. A less severe reaction may present with facial swelling, hives, or itchiness.

If you suspect your Siamese cat has a food allergy, it is vital that you talk to your vet to identify the cause. Allergies tend to last a lifetime, so the ingredient will need to be removed permanently from your cat's diet.

Food sensitivities occur without an immune component. They can easily be managed and often will disappear over time. If you suspect your cat has a food intolerance, talk to your vet; look for a hypoallergenic food that avoids common allergens, such as beef or wheat, and choose a cat food with a single protein source.

Human Foods to Avoid

Slipping your Siamese cat, a morsel or two under the table may be tempting, but it can cause your feline cat some serious health issues or even be fatal. You might be surprised at some of the foods your furry friend needs to avoid at all costs!

Alcohol – Even the tiniest amount of any type of alcohol can be fatal for your Siamese cat. Alcohol causes cats to have coordination problems, vomiting, diarrhea, breathing issues, and even death.

Caffeine – All types of caffeine are fatal for your cat, including cocoa, energy drinks, guarana, tea, caffeinated carbonated beverages, and soda. If your cat accidentally consumes a product with caffeine, go immediately to the nearest veterinarian's office.

Chocolate – Dark, white, and milk chocolate are deadly for cats. Even the smallest morsel can cause diarrhea, vomiting, cardiac failure, seizures, and even death.

Citrus fruits – Citrus fruits like oranges, lemons, limes, tangerines, and grapefruits contain citric acid and essential oils that can cause problems in cats. The stems, leaves, peels, fruits, and seeds should be avoided. Small amounts will only cause tummy upset, but large amounts can cause diarrhea, vomiting, and central nervous system depression.

Coconut flesh and coconut water – Fresh coconut milk and flesh can cause digestive issues in cats. Coconut water is too high in potassium to be safe for cats, though coconut oil may be helpful for some skin issues. Talk to your vet before using this as a topical or holistic remedy or including it in your cat's diet.

Dairy products – Dairy products such as milk, whipped cream, and ice cream can cause your kitty to experience digestive discomfort and diarrhea. Many cats who are lactose intolerant have extremely itchy skin. That said, the majority of cats can tolerate cheese and yogurt due to the natural digestive enzymes and probiotics.

Grapes or raisins – Grapes and raisins seem the perfect bite-sized treat for your cat, but a few can cause kidney failure. If you think your Siamese cat may have consumed some grapes or raisins, call your veterinarian if you notice any sluggish behavior or severe vomiting.

Nuts – Macadamia nuts are toxic for cats. Macadamia nuts cause vomiting, muscle tremors, fever, and loss of muscle control. Eating chocolate-covered macadamia nuts will intensify the symptoms, which will eventually lead to death. Other types of nuts, such as almonds, pecans, and walnuts, can cause digestive issues and potentially even pancreatitis.

Some vegetables and herbs – Though cats can eat some vegetables, onions, garlic, leeks, scallions, shallots, and chives are particularly harmful to cats, causing gastrointestinal distress and even damage to the red blood cells. Foods containing these vegetables and herbs, such as garlic bread, should be avoided as well.

Raw eggs – Raw eggs are a source of bacteria, such as salmonella or E. coli. Avoid feeding your Siamese cat raw or undercooked eggs or any type of raw animal products, such as fish, beef, pork, or chicken.

Raw yeast dough – Before baking, yeast dough needs to rise. If your Siamese cat eats some raw dough, it will continue to rise inside her stomach, stretching out your cat's abdomen, causing extreme pain. The yeast can also cause alcohol poisoning.

Salt – A word of caution: do not share your salted popcorn or pretzels with your furry friend.

Too much salt can cause sodium poisoning, vomiting, diarrhea, fever, or seizures and may be fatal if left untreated.

Xylitol – Xylitol is a common sweetener used in baked goods, toothpaste, and diet products. It causes your cat's blood sugar levels to drop, which leads to liver failure.

If your Siamese cat got into the pantry and ate something she shouldn't have, call your local vet immediately or call the Animal Poison Control Center (ASPCA) at (888) 426-4435.

Thankfully, since cats are such fussy eaters, it is very rare for a cat to have food-related toxicosis. Typically, it is more of a problem with dogs, who are more adventurous and undiscriminating with regards to what they eat. Before making any changes to your cat's diet, talk to your vet about what ingredients are safe and what amounts are safe for your cat.

It is not advisable to make a practice out of giving your Siamese cat leftovers, bits of meat, or other scraps, as she may begin to refuse to eat her normal food. Also, it can unbalance your cat's regular diet, causing her to gain weight. Human foods can cause gas, which may not be a problem for your kitty, but it could be for you!

After all that talk about harmful human foods for your cat, you are probably wondering: "Is all human food bad for my cat?" Although you may use great self-control to keep your Siamese cat on her canine diet, sometimes you may not be able to resist the urge to slip her a piece of cooked chicken.

Before giving your cat any foods that are not on this list, do some research to make sure they are safe. If your kitty experiences any sort of reaction or allergy, immediately consult a veterinarian. Here are some of the best human food choices for your four-pawed furry friend:

Cooked chicken or turkey – Cooked chicken is a healthy source of protein and makes a great alternative to high-calorie treats used in obedience training. Plus, if you accidentally run out of cat food, it makes a healthy meal replacement.

Yogurt – Yogurt is high in calcium and protein. Also, its active probiotics can aid your cat's digestive system and improve her breath.

Salmon – Salmon is an excellent source of omega-3 fatty acids, which will help keep your Siamese cat's coat healthy and shiny and support her immune system. Try adding cooked salmon to your cat's kibble, or slip her some unwanted fish skins.

Oatmeal – Cooked oatmeal is an excellent source of soluble fiber, which is especially beneficial to senior cats with bowel irregularity issues. It is a fantastic grain option for cats allergic to wheat. Always cook oatmeal before serving it to your cat, and only use oatmeal that has no added sugar or additives.

Cheese – Cheese is an excellent snack for your feline friend if she is not lactose intolerant. Choose low-fat varieties and do not overfeed, as most cheeses are high in fat and may cause constipation. Cottage cheese is typically a good option for Siamese cats.

Pumpkin – Pumpkins are part of the squash family, all of which are excellent sources of fiber, beta carotene, and vitamin A. Plus, pumpkin can keep your kitty's GI tract moving and aid with digestive issues.

Eggs – A scrambled egg will give your Siamese cat's diet a protein boost. Eggs are remarkably high in protein and a source of digestible riboflavin and selenium. Always thoroughly cook the eggs to avoid any risk of salmonella.

Apple slices – Sliced apples are high in fiber and vitamins and are a healthy treat for your feline friend. Additionally, apple slices are known for cleaning cats' teeth and freshening their breath. Before giving your cat a few apple slices, make sure to remove the skin, seeds, and the core, as they can be a choking hazard.

If you decide to give your kitty a treat or two from your table, make sure it is not seasoned, fatty, salty, or raw. Certain fruits, such as thin slices of apples, bananas, or watermelon, all make yummy treats for your Siamese cat. Be sure to remove any seeds, peels, or stems that could get stuck in your cat's digestive tract.

When introducing your kitty to a new food, do not be surprised if she is a little finicky about what she eats. Give your cat a variety of options to see what she likes, and make sure to do everything in moderation. Make sure your cat is receiving her proper nutritional needs by feeding her cat food in addition to any human food snacks.

Cooked, plain white rice or noodles with a piece of boiled chicken might be the best solution if your kitty has an upset tummy.

Commercial Cat Food

In the last few years, commercial cat food has improved enormously. A few decades ago, there were only a few generic brands of cat food on the shelves, whereas today, you can find countless brands, which cater to different breeds, ages, and dietary restrictions. However, with so many choices out there, it can be overwhelming to narrow down what type of cat food is best suited for your Siamese cat.

Learning about how commercial cat food is made will help you understand the nutritional value of the food you are feeding your Siamese cat. There are two main types of commercially prepared cat food: canned food and dry kibble. Commercially produced fresh cat food is a newcomer to the cat food aisle and is quickly gaining popularity but is not yet widely available.

Wet cat food

Wet cat food may be sold in cans, boxes, or single-serving pouches, often consisting of 35–75 percent water, depending on the quality. Be sure to look for the moisture content on the label. Wet foods contain a variety of meats such as beef, chicken, lamb, salmon, or venison.

Once the can or package is opened, it must be refrigerated to maintain its freshness, and most cats will refuse to eat cold food. To solve this problem, you can warm up the meal portion before serving. Note that wet foods have the highest cost per serving, and cheaper brands of wet food are high in fillers, sugar, and fat.

Wet cat food is made using fresh and frozen meat. Many commercial brands use animal parts such as organs or fatty tissue. One of the advantages of these parts is they have a higher nutritional value than meats typically consumed by humans. The meat is then ground and mixed in large machines to ensure even distribution of the calories and nutrients.

The packaging method used for wet food uses a high heat sterilization method to kill off any bacteria, but an unwanted side effect is that it also destroys the nutrients and vitamins. The sterilization and vacuum-sealing process ensure a longer shelf life without the need to use harmful chemicals.

However, due to the processing method, wet foods are notorious for being void of nutrients. If you want your cat to get her daily nutritional requirements, you will need to give her a huge portion at each meal, which will eventually result in weight gain. For this very reason, most vets recommend feeding your cat wet and dry food.

HELPFUL TIP
How Much Protein?

Like other cats, Siamese cats are natural carnivores and require a large amount of protein from meat. Plant-based protein isn't ideal for cats since they can only get certain amino acids, such as taurine, from meat sources. A good rule of thumb when determining how much protein your Siamese cat needs is to feed approximately two grams of protein per pound of body weight per day. Different meats contain different protein levels, so be sure to check this when feeding your cat.

Dry cat food

The majority of cats throughout the United States are fed dry kibble.

Dry cat food contains similar ingredients as wet cat food, but instead of adding gravy and canning the product, the meat mixture is pulverized and mixed together to create a consistent mass of dough that can then be cooked. The dough can be manufactured by one of the following methods:

Baked – The dough is extruded through specially shaped holes and then baked at a low temperature. Once baked, the kibble is left out to dry and then sprayed with fats, oils, minerals, and vitamins. Often, baked kibble contains wheat gluten to aid in binding the ingredients together.

Cold-pressed – This is a newbie in the cat food aisle that is quickly gaining popularity with both pet owners and cats alike. Cold-pressed cat food often prides itself on only using the freshest of ingredients. The manufacturer grinds the ingredients together, forming a thick, coarse paste, which is then left to dry before being pressed out to remove the excess moisture. It is then baked at a very low temperature to prevent any nutrient loss.

Extrusion – This method is similar to baking, except before extruding the dough through specially shaped holes, the mixture is first cooked in huge steam and pressure cookers to kill off any bacteria, etc. Then, when the mixture cools, it is pressed through an extruding machine, shaping the kibble. After this, the kibble is placed into a high-heat convection oven to remove any excess moisture.

It is worth mentioning that this type of kibble's double exposure to extreme heat removes the majority of the nutrients and vitamins.

Freeze dried – The fresh food is mixed together, then ground into a coarse paste, formed into small pieces of kibble, and placed inside a type of vacuum oven that removes all excess moisture. The process preserves the majority of the nutrients, making it one of the healthiest food choices for your Siamese cat.

Freeze-dried foods have a long shelf life without the need for harmful preservatives. Some freeze-dried foods may need to be rehydrated with water before serving. This is one of the most expensive dry cat food options.

Fresh cat food

Fresh cat food is quickly gaining popularity in the pet food aisle. Fresh cat food manufacturers pride themselves on using only fresh, organic ingredients and human-grade proteins. Many companies provide the option of using recyclable, reusable serving trays.

One of the main advantages of fresh cat food is its high nutritional value due to the low level of processing required. On the other hand, since it does contain preservatives, fresh food has a maximum life span of seven to 14 days and will need to be stored in the refrigerator. It is not recommended to freeze fresh cat food, as many of the nutrients will be lost.

As cats are finicky eaters, they might not like the texture or temperature of fresh food. You may have to experiment with a few different brands until you find the brand your cat will gobble up.

Wet cat food vs. dry cat food

As you can see above, both wet and dry cat food can be good choices, depending on the quality of ingredients and the process used to manufacture the cat food. However, they each offer different benefits and drawbacks depending on your Siamese cat's nutritional needs.

Benefits of wet cat food compared to dry cat food

- **Higher moisture content** - Your veterinarian may recommend a wet cat food diet if your cat frequently suffers from urinary tract infections or dislikes drinking water.
- **Palatability** - Wet cat food is preferred by cats who are finicky eaters. Also, wet cat food is ideal for concealing medications. It is ideal for elderly or sick cats whose appetite has decreased.
- **Easier to chew** - Cats who have dental issues or other oral abnormalities may find eating wet food easier than dry food.
- **Satiety** - Wet cat food tends to cause a longer-lasting feeling of being full. Increased satiety is especially useful in managing your cat's weight.

Benefits of dry cat food compared to wet cat food

- **Dental health** - One of the main advantages to dry food is that it acts like a toothbrush, helping to remove and prevent the buildup of plaque and tartar on your cat's teeth.
- **Convenience and cost-effectiveness** - Kibble's popularity is due to the convenience for feeding and cost (as with most things, the larger the

bag, the better the savings). In addition, it stays fresh longer than wet foods once the package has been opened.

- **Food enrichment** – Kibble is easy to use with food puzzles that help to keep your cat mentally stimulated and improve the quality of her life.

As you can see, there are quite a few factors to take into consideration when choosing the best cat food for your Siamese cat. Ultimately, choosing the right cat food is a very personal decision and depends on your budget and personal preferences. The right cat food for your Siamese cat will meet her nutritional requirements and keep her happy and healthy.

How to Read Cat Food Labels

Cat food nutrition labels are similar to the nutrition facts on packaged food for humans. The labels are designed to help you compare products and learn more about what you are considering purchasing and feeding your cat.

Quick tip: Look past the attractive packaging and marketing; instead, learn to read the ingredients.

General rule of thumb: If humans are not allowed to eat it, then you should not feed it to your cat either.

Just as with packaged food for humans, cat food must list the ingredients according to weight, starting with the heaviest. A word of caution: if the first ingredient is a protein, keep in mind that proteins are typically about 75 percent water.

Cat food labels are required to contain:

- Product brand name
- Quantity displayed in terms of weight, liquid measure, or count, depending on the formulation of the cat food
- Ingredients listed in descending order by weight
- Feeding instructions for your cat's age, activity level, and weight
- Nutritional statement backed up by research and testing to prove the food provides the required daily nutritional requirements
- Manufacturer's name and address
- Calorie statement and the life stages the food is appropriate for

Continue reading to learn which ingredients to avoid and why they can harm your Siamese cat's health.

Artificial preservatives - Avoid cat foods that contain ethoxyquin, BHA, and BHT on the ingredient list. The National Institute of Health has deemed BHA and BHT to be carcinogenic and unfit for human consumption. Ethoxyquin is linked to cancer, chronic immune diseases, and kidney failure in both humans and animals.

Corn and rice fillers - Corn and rice fillers are commonly used for fattening up animals, and the last thing your Siamese needs is a carbohydrate-rich diet. A low-protein diet is one of the main causes of obesity in smaller felines, such as your Siamese cat. A diet high in corn and rice can cause chronic digestive issues, such as bloating, gas, and diarrhea.

Food coloring - Many cat food manufacturers add food coloring to their kibble and/or treats to make them look more appealing and appetizing. But your Siamese cat is not concerned about the appearance or color of her food; she just cares whether it is tasty. Avoid cat foods that contain food dyes such as Blue 2, Red 40, or Yellow 5 because they are linked to allergies, hyperactivity, and cancer.

MSG - Monosodium glutamate (MSG) is a well-known flavor enhancer for Chinese food and cat food. MSG overstimulates your cat's brain, causing her to produce a hormone called dopamine, making her become addicted to her food. Recent studies have shown that when pets regularly consume foods with MSG, they can develop brain damage, obesity, and behavioral issues.

Nondescript fats - Fat is essential for your Siamese cat's overall health. Many manufacturers of cat food list generic animal fat as one of the ingredients, which often is fat derived from sick or rancid animals. Choose a cat food that specifies the type of fat used, such as salmon fat instead of fish fat or coconut oil instead of vegetable oil, etc.

Propylene glycol - Propylene glycol is a common ingredient in antifreeze and is extremely toxic for cats. However, many cat food manufacturers add it to their products to reduce moisture from building up inside of the packaging, prevent bacterial growth, and lengthen the product's life span.

Rendered foods - Rendered meat is often listed on the ingredient list as animal by-product meal, which is a mix of animal parts such as blood, brains, spleens, entrails, and internal organs. Often, it includes discarded animal parts that were considered to be unfit for human consumption. The nutritional value of rendered meat is extremely low and can be a source of salmonella and toxins.

Sugar - Many cat foods contain sugar to mask a bitter flavor and to improve texture. Once your Siamese cat is addicted to sugar, it is extremely difficult to switch her to a healthier, sugar-free alternative. Sugar additives to watch out for are cane sugar, beet pulp, corn syrup, sucrose, fructose-glucose, xylitol, molasses, and sorbitol.

Some cat owners shy away from buying food that contains synthetic preservatives such as BHA (butylated hydroxyanisole), BHT (butylated hydroxytoluene), or ethoxyquin. These synthetic preservatives prevent fat from turning rancid and can keep dry cat food fresh for at least a year. The FDA has approved these preservatives as safe for animals in small amounts.

Ethoxyquin came under scrutiny after a long list of complaints concerning some pets who were given food with this preservative, such as skin allergies, reproductive problems, cancer, and organ failure. The FDA requested pet food manufacturers reduce the amount of ethoxyquin to half of the previously approved amount.

Some pet food manufacturers have opted to use natural preservatives like vitamin E (mixed tocopherols), vitamin C (ascorbic acid), and plant extracts such as rosemary. These natural preservatives help to keep dry food fresh but for a shortened life span. Be sure to check your cat food bag for the "best by" date on the label before buying or feeding it to your Siamese cat.

DECIPHERING TERMS

Recently there have been so many new trends in the cat food market that it can be challenging to decipher the terms. Here are some terms that can be difficult to understand:

Organic – As of the moment this book went to print, the US Department of Agriculture (USDA) was still developing official regulations regarding the labeling of organic foods for pets. In the meantime, cat foods that claim to be organic must meet the requirements established by the USDA's National Organic Program, which means organic cat food has to meet the same standards as organic human food.

Organic cat food must contain no artificial sweeteners, preservatives, flavorings, or food colorings. Plus, meat and meat by-products must be sourced from animals with no antibiotics or growth hormones. Generally speaking, cats with sensitive tummies do better on an organic diet.

Note: "natural" cat food is not the same as "organic." The term "natural cat food" refers to the lack of artificial ingredients used in the product.

Grain-free – Recent studies by the FDA have discovered grain-free cat foods are linked to feline dilated cardiomyopathy (CDC), which causes the cat's heart to enlarge and prevents the blood from circulating freely throughout the body. The FDA recommends pet owners avoid feeding their cats grain-free foods. Cats need a diet based on high-quality proteins, natural fats, vegetables, and whole grains to meet their dietary needs.

Another disadvantage to a grain-free diet is that it contains other forms of carbohydrates, such as potatoes, peas, or lentils. Some of these carbohydrates can cause your cat gastrointestinal upset.

New proteins – This term refers to new meats in the cat food market, such as bison, kangaroo, rabbit, lamb, and other exotic animals. At the moment, it is difficult to rate the benefits of this food due to a lack of research on the different nutrient profiles when compared with common proteins, such as beef, chicken, or fish.

Human-grade cat food – This is defined as legally edible and safe for human consumption. Human-grade cat food is tightly regulated by the FDA and the USDA. Also, the Association of American Feed Control Officials (AAFCO) requires that human-grade cat food be manufactured, packaged, and held in accordance with federal regulations for human food.

Light, low-calorie, and low-fat – If labeled with one of these terms, cat food must have a significant reduction in fat or calories when compared to the brand's standard cat food. The AAFCO requires that any cat food label claiming to be light, low-calorie, or low-fat must show the reduction on the label and name the product in comparison.

Good foods to watch out for

Finding a wholesome, healthy, and delicious food for your Siamese cat may seem like a challenge, but it is not impossible. When choosing a cat food for your cat, look for a variety of ingredients such as meat, veggies, grains, and fruits. Look for some of the following ingredients on the nutrition label:

Meat – Your Siamese cat is a high-energy cat who needs plenty of healthy proteins to maintain her body, muscle, and immune system. Look for commercial cat foods made from human-grade proteins, such as beef, chicken, salmon, rabbit, etc.

Whole-meat meal – Often, meat meal is from by-products such as rendered meats, whereas whole-meat meal is a high source of protein and is simply a fancier way of saying ground beef. However, the ingredient list should specify the type of whole meat meal used, such as chicken, beef, etc. Meat meal contains more protein, as it is ground up, then dried to a 10 percent moisture level, making the protein level at least 65 percent and at least 12 percent fat.

Carbohydrates and grains – Whole grains are an exceptional source of energy for your Siamese cat, and they improve her digestion. Avoid cat foods made from corn, soy, or white rice; instead, look for higher-quality ingredients, such as brown rice, whole oats, barley, and peas. Carbohydrates and grains should never be one of the first ingredients on the list.

Vegetables and fruits – Both provide essential nutrients, minerals, vitamins, fiber, and antioxidants. For example, sweet potatoes are an excellent source of potassium, vitamin B, and antioxidants. Unsweetened cranberries provide vitamin C, prevent urinary tract infections, and protect your kitty's teeth from harmful bacteria.

Fats – Fats are necessary for your Siamese cat's overall health, proper cell function, and digestion. Fats help your Siamese cat absorb minerals and vitamins and keep her coat and teeth in tip-top shape. Look for cat foods that contain wholesome fats like omega-3 and omega-6 fatty acids, canola oil, salmon fat, and olive oils.

CAUTION:

- *Pay attention to the product name, as it will give you a clue about the ingredients in the cat food you are considering. Most cat owners base their decision on a specific ingredient. Many brands will highlight that ingredient in the product's label.*
- *Stay away from commercial cat foods that use the term "with," such as "with chicken" or "with beef." Manufacturers are only required to use 3 percent of protein in the cat food. Avoid cat food whose labels include the wording "flavor," such as beef or chicken flavor, as this indicates it was made with an exceedingly small percentage of the actual product and mostly contains artificial flavoring.*
- *Just because a cat food manufacturer claims to provide everything your Siamese cat needs for her optimum health does not necessarily mean the food is really healthy. Take the time to carefully read the ingredient list and make a decision based on the ingredients, not based on the attractive packaging.*

Weight Management

- Losing weight is tough on anyone — two- or four-legged! Helping your feline friend shed those extra pounds is easier than you think. It simply requires discipline and commitment on your part and the assistance of your veterinary healthcare team.

Cats, like people, have a harder time getting around if they are overweight. Losing weight can be a challenge for cats at any age, but even more so as they get older. Despite the challenges, weight loss for cats of any age is worth the effort. Slender cats enjoy longer lives, show fewer visible signs of aging, and have fewer chances of developing feline arthritis.

As little as one pound above your Siamese cat's ideal weight can put your cat at risk of developing serious medical conditions. Unfortunately, if your cat is overweight or obese, it is no longer a question if she will develop a secondary condition caused by excess weight, but how soon and how serious. Some common health problems associated with excess weight include:

- Type 2 diabetes
- Heart disease
- Osteoarthritis (arthritis)
- High blood pressure
- Increased frequency of joint injuries
- Some forms of cancer

If you cannot feel your Siamese cat's ribs and shoulder blades, if her waist is not discernible (a tuck behind her ribs), or if there is a roll of fat at the base of her tail, then it is time to face reality and put your kitty on a diet.

If in doubt, ask your vet for his professional opinion about your cat's weight.

How should I begin a weight loss program for my cat?

Theoretically, weight loss seems straightforward — fewer calories equal weight loss. Unfortunately, it is not as simple as that. You should never put your obese cat on a diet without strict veterinary supervision.

Cats' physiology is very different from humans and dogs, and if they do not eat for two consecutive days, they can develop a life-threatening form of liver disease called hepatic lipidosis (also called fatty liver syndrome).

Your veterinarian will examine your Siamese cat to make sure she has no underlying conditions that may hinder your cat's weight loss. Then, your veterinarian will determine your cat's ideal body weight based on body size and build. Your veterinarian will determine the number of calories your cat requires daily to safely achieve her ideal weight. The amount of food will depend on the caloric value of the food you are planning to feed your cat.

For most cats, the best way to lose weight is with a canned diet, fed several times per day, rather than leaving food out all day long. One of the reasons wet or canned food is preferable for weight loss is because even the fussiest cats will eat it.

Treats and rewards often have three to five calories, and they can quickly add up. Instead of store-bought treats, try using pieces of cut-up skinless chicken breast. Most cats are more concerned about the number of treats they are receiving and do not notice the size of the actual treat, so cut up chewy treats into smaller pieces.

How can I get my cat to exercise more?

In an ideal world, we would take our cats for a walk around the block, but we do not live in that world. Cats evolved as stalkers who expend as little energy as possible in seeking out their prey. When cats come across prey, they burst into a short pursuit. Most wild cats pursue their prey at top speed for less than a minute. Once the pursuit is over, they require hours to recover for the next hunt.

Your Siamese cat is simply a smaller version of these wild felines. For this reason, you will need to use your ingenuity to convince your chunky kitty to move around a little more. Here are some simple ideas:

- Attempt moving your cat's food bowl to different locations in your house, such as upstairs or downstairs. Be sure to regularly rotate the food dish so that your cat has to walk around looking for it.
- Cats tend to sleep and lounge near their food dish so that they do not have to walk too far for a snack. Try moving the dish further away from your feline's typical resting spots.
- Instead of using a feeding bowl, place the dry kibble in special feeding balls that require your cat to roll the ball around to get food as a reward.
- Set aside playtime with your cat. Play a game of hide-and-seek or use feather or laser toys to get your cat moving.

How to Keep Your Siamese Hydrated

The average Siamese cat needs approximately one ounce of water per pound of body weight every day. So, if your feline friend weighs eight pounds, she will need approximately eight ounces or one cup of water each day. However, this is just an estimate and varies depending on each cat's activity level, the temperature of the cat's environment, and his or her unique physical needs.

Siamese cats are very particular and prefer fresh water, so do not just add water to the bowl in which the level has dropped. Dump out the entire bowl, wash out the slime from the bottom of the bowl, and fill it with fresh, clean water. Ask yourself: if you are thirsty, do you use a half-filled glass out of the sink, or do you reach for a clean glass from your cupboard and fill it with fresh, clean water?

Cats are curious by nature. Take advantage of your cat's curiosity by placing water in different types of containers and in different places around the house. By doing this, you are not only encouraging your cat to drink more water but also providing her with mental stimulation.

Pet water fountains are another fantastic option to encourage your cat to drink more water. Siamese cats are fascinated by flowing water, so it may encourage more drinking. In addition to providing a fresh source of drinking water, pet fountains are more environmentally friendly than leaving the faucet running. But just like your cat's water dish, water fountains need to be cleaned regularly.

Felines evolved to get hydration from food rather than from drinking water, and wet food can help ensure your cat receives enough water every day. Non-gravy wet foods tend to be lower in carbohydrates than dry cat foods, so regularly feeding your cat wet food may help her maintain a healthy weight. You can even add a tablespoon of fresh water or diluted broth to the wet food to further increase the amount of water your cat is consuming.

Occasionally adding a small amount of low-sodium broth (chicken or beef) to your cat's water bowl can tempt your cat to drink more. If you live in a warmer climate, throw a frozen cube of broth into your cat's water.

Signs your cat may be dehydrated

There are a few signs that your cat may be dehydrated:

- Dry gums
- Lethargy
- Loss of appetite
- Sunken eyes
- Decreased skin elasticity
- Urinating less frequently

If your cat becomes dehydrated, she can develop serious electrolyte imbalances, which reduce the flow of blood and oxygen to body organs. Plus, your Siamese cat may begin to accumulate harmful toxins in the body. Improper water consumption may lead to your feline friend feeling lethargic, having poor skin health, and could increase the risk for urethral obstruction in male cats.

CHAPTER 10

Grooming Your Siamese

Good grooming helps your Siamese cat feel and look her best. Regular grooming removes loose fur and dirt. It also smooths out mats and tangles and redistributes the natural oils. Siamese cats can have 130,000 hairs covering their body, so it is not surprising they could use a little help keeping their coat healthy. Plus, routine grooming sessions give you an opportunity to examine your cat's coat, eyes, teeth, ears, and nails for any health problems.

Brushing

A clean cat is a happy cat!

Brushing your Siamese cat not only removes dirt, grease, and dead hair from her coat, but it also helps to remove skin flakes and stimulates blood circulation, improving the overall condition of her skin.

How to brush your cat – Preferably using a fine-toothed metal comb, work the brush through your cat's fur from head to tail to remove dirt and debris. Work along her fur; never brush in the opposite direction the fur grows. Brush all over your cat's body, including her chest and abdomen. A rubber brush can be very effective in removing dead hair and tangles.

If you have a hard time remembering to brush your Siamese cat daily, place the brushes in a place where you will see them, such as beside the television remote.

All cats shed, and your Siamese cat is no exception. Excessive shedding can easily be prevented by providing your cat with a healthy diet, plenty of exercise, and fresh air. If you notice while brushing your cat that she is losing more hair than normal, the cause may be one of the following factors:

- Hot spots
- Sarcoptic mange

- Food-related allergies
- Parasites, such as fleas, lice, or mites
- An immune disorder, such as adrenal or thyroid diseases
- Cancer
- Anxiety or stress
- Pregnancy or lactation
- A bacterial or fungal infection, such as ringworm

If your Siamese cat goes outside, you will need to check her daily for ticks. In the following chapter, we will discuss how to remove a tick.

As you brush your kitten, look for sores, rashes, or signs of infection such as redness, swelling, skin inflammation, and tenderness. The same is true if you notice any patches of dry, brittle skin.

If you notice any foreign objects lodged in your cat's eyes, ears, skin, mouth, or paw pads, do not attempt to remove them yourself — always consult with your veterinarian beforehand.

If matted hair is an issue, leave your household scissors in the drawer where they belong. One wrong movement by a nervous cat could result in an injury to you or your feline friend. The best way to remove a knot or mat is by using your fingers, some pet-friendly conditioner, a comb, and a whole lot of patience.

Neglecting to brush your feline friend's coat can lead to painful tangles and hairballs. When your Siamese cat is suffering from hairballs, she will cough them up on the floor or expel them in her fecal matter. If, despite regular brushing, your cat continues to have hairballs, talk to your veterinarian for a recommended solution.

HELPFUL TIP

The Perfect Brush

Finding the perfect brush for your short-haired Siamese cat can be a process of trial and error. However, you can narrow your search to a few types of brushes that are most popular with owners of this breed. One of the best brushes for Siamese cats is a short-bristled slicker brush, which can remove mats and loose hair. Another popular option is rubber-bristled brushes that remove dead hair and distribute your cat's natural oils through his coat. Rubber-bristled brushes may come in the form of a brush or even be attached to gloves.

Bathing

Your Siamese cat has built-in grooming tools with her tongue and teeth. But if she gets into something smelly or sticky, you may have to bathe her occasionally. Follow these steps to ensure minimal stress and maximum efficiency:

- Schedule bath time when your cat is most mellow, perhaps after a play session with a toy of her choice.
- For your own protection, I highly recommend trimming your kitty's claws before bathing.
- Before bathing, thoroughly brush your cat to remove any loose hair and tangles.
- Gently place some cotton balls in her ears to keep the water out.
- Place a rubber mat inside the sink or basin where you will be bathing your cat so that she does not slip. Fill the sink or basin with three to four inches of lukewarm water.
- Use a hand-held sprayer to thoroughly wet your kitty, taking care not to directly spray her eyes, ears, or nose. If you do not have a spray hose, use a plastic pitcher.
- Gently massage the cat shampoo into your cat's fur, working from the head to the tip of her tail, in the direction of the hair growth. Take care to avoid your cat's eyes, nose, and ears.
- Thoroughly rinse the shampoo off your cat using a spray hose with lukewarm water or a pitcher. Be sure all the residue shampoo has been removed, as it can irritate your cat's skin and act as a magnet for dirt.
- Use a soft washcloth to wipe your cat's face. Plain water should be fine unless her face is very dirty — in which case, I recommend using diluted cat shampoo, being very cautious around your cat's eyes and nose.
- Wrap your cat in an oversized towel and dry her in a warm place, away from drafts. If your cat does not mind the noise, you can use a hairdryer on the lowest heat setting.
- Reward your Siamese cat with praise and a few of her favorite treats when the bathing ordeal is over.

Never spray your cat with scents or perfumes. Cats are very sensitive to fragrances, and most fragrances contain harmful ingredients that can make your cat very sick if she ingests them while cleaning herself. Fragrances can also result in respiratory problems. The best way to keep your Siamese cat smelling sweet is by regularly bathing her.

Photo Courtesy of Nausheen Kasmani

Just a reminder – Never ever use human shampoo or conditioner to wash your Siamese cat, as it contains chemicals and fragrances that may irritate her skin. Instead, choose a high-quality shampoo specifically formulated for cats. Avoid using inexpensive cat shampoos as they often are made with harsh ingredients.

Nail Clipping

> *Be sure to trim nails weekly for the first year as the nails grow quickly. By trimming weekly, your kitten will become used to this activity and will not give you a hard time. Remember, cats cannot trim their own nails. You must be responsible for this. After the first year, a biweekly trim is adequate. In all cases, just take off the pointy tip, 1 or 3 mm. That's it.*
>
> CAROL GAGATCH
> *Carolina Blues Cattery*

Siamese cats need healthy feet to scratch, climb, and achieve their famed acrobat landings. Most Siamese cats are squeamish about having their nails trimmed and instantly disappear the minute those nail clippers come into sight.

Chances are your Siamese cat's nails will need to be trimmed every ten to fourteen days or so, unless she is running around on hard surfaces such as cement that keep her nails short. A general rule of thumb: if you can hear your cat's nails clicking against the floor or her nails get snagged on the carpet, then it is time for a trim.

If possible, get your Siamese cat used to having her nails clipped at a young age by rubbing your hands up and down her legs and gently pressing down between her toes each time. Never forget to give your kitty a yummy treat, followed by a big, boisterous, "Good girl!" After about two weeks of massaging your Siamese cat's feet, you can attempt to clip her nails. This method works especially well if your older cat is ticklish or wary about having her feet touched.

Get your cat used to the sound of the clippers before you attempt to trim her nails. If your kitty sniffs the clippers, place a yummy treat on top for her to eat. Sit her on your lap, put a piece of uncooked spaghetti into the clippers, and hold them near to your cat. While massaging your cat's feet, press gently on the pad of her feet and when the nail extends, clip the spaghetti in the clippers. Now release her toe and give her a treat and praise. Repeat until your cat doesn't squirm at the sound of the clippers.

If you are unsure about how to cut your Siamese cat's nails, ask your veterinarian or groomer; they will gladly give you a short demonstration on how to trim her nails to the right length.

There are two different types of nail clippers — scissor-type and guillotine. Both styles come highly recommended, so choose the style you feel the most comfortable with. Another option is a nail grinder, which sands the nails down; however, it makes a loud, grinding noise, and the vibration can frighten you and your cat.

Photo Courtesy of Joshua & Christian Wallace

Follow these steps to help your cat relax while you trim:

- Choose a chair in a quiet room where you can comfortably hold your cat on your lap. Take care that your kitty cannot spy any birds fluttering or animal action outside nearby windows — and be sure there are no other pets in the room.
- Choose a moment when your cat is relaxed and even sleepy, such as in the middle of a deep afternoon nap.
- Snip off the tip of the nail, avoiding the quick. The quick is the darker-colored circle inside of the nail, which is the blood vein. If you accidentally cut the quick, you will have one very unhappy cat.
- If you accidentally cut your Siamese cat's nail quick, use a nail cauterizer, such as cornstarch or styptic powder, which you can apply with a Q-Tip. Be sure to have a moist washcloth on hand to clean up the mess. Cutting your cat's nail quick hurts, and trust me — she will remember this unpleasant experience for a long time.
- Do not attempt to trim all your cat's nails in one sitting. If your cat resists or tries to pull away, do not raise your voice or punish her. Never attempt nail clipping when you or your cat are upset.

If you are using a nail grinder to trim your Siamese cat's nails, follow the method above; simply hold your cat's foot and grind a little off each nail. This method may take your cat longer to get used to due to the loud grinding noise.

Do not forget to trim your Siamese cat's dewclaws. Since they do not touch the ground, they tend to grow longer and will eventually grow back into your cat's paw, which can be very painful and may cause health complications.

If your Siamese cat has darker nails, you will need to be extra careful because it is almost impossible to notice the nail quick. If you have a hard time keeping your hands steady or your cat shows aggressive behavior while getting her nails clipped, feel free to ask the groomer to clip her nails for you.

Why You Should Never Declaw Your Siamese

Too often, people assume that declawing is a simple procedure that removes the cat's nail or is the equivalent of having your fingernails trimmed. Sadly, nothing could be further from the truth.

Declawing involves amputating the final part of the last bone of each toe. If performed on a human being, it would be like cutting off each finger at the last knuckle.

This is unnecessary surgery that provides zero medical benefits to your cat. Educated cat owners can easily train their cats to claw only in specific areas, such as a scratching post.

Scratching is normal behavior for cats. Cats scratch to remove the dead husks from their claws, mark territory, de-stress, and stretch their muscles. Declawing your cat can actually lead to an entirely different set of behavior problems that may be worse than shredding the couch. For example, a declawed cat is less likely to use the litter box and more likely to bite.

Declawing can also cause lasting physical problems for your cat, such as constant pain in the paws, infections, tissue necrosis (tissue death), lameness, and back pain. Removing the claw changes the way the cat's foot hits the ground and can cause pain similar to wearing a poorly fitting pair of shoes. There can also be regrowth of improperly removed claws, nerve damage, and bone spurs.

Many countries have banned declawing. The Humane Society of the United States opposes declawing except in the rare occurrence when the cat needs it for a medical purpose, such as the removal of cancerous nail bed tumors.

Importance of Good Dental Care

> *One of the most important care tips for a Siamese is dental care... brushing the teeth/gums. Some Siamese are binge eaters; they swallow their food whole and don't chew the kibble. Chewing massages the gums, thus preventing gingivitis. Those who are bingers will need oral care regularly to prevent gingivitis.*
>
> KAREN SPOHN
> *Candi Dasa cattery*

Your Siamese cat needs clean, sharp teeth and healthy gums. Cats can develop dental issues such as tartar, plaque, and gingivitis. As if bad breath was not enough, these feline dental problems can lead to life-threatening infections, not to mention dental extractions, which can be very costly to treat. The only way to prevent this is by practicing good oral care.

Since your kitty cannot brush her teeth on her own, you will need to brush her teeth regularly. Older cats can learn to be comfortable getting their teeth brushed, but you can make things easier for yourself by starting early with your cat when she is still a kitten.

Get your kitten used to having her teeth cleaned by gently massaging her gums for about 20 to 30 seconds daily for about two weeks. Once she is comfortable with you touching her gum line, do the same procedure daily but including her teeth for another two weeks.

Brush your cat's teeth at home by following these simple steps:

1. Place a pea-sized amount of feline toothpaste on the tip of your finger, then let your cat smell it and taste it.
2. Gently massage the toothpaste onto her gums. This will allow her to get used to the texture and the flavor.
3. Use a double-headed feline toothbrush (which looks similar to a Q-Tip) held at a 45-degree angle to clean below the gumline.
4. Work on one spot at a time until your Siamese cat gets used to the feel of the toothbrush inside of her mouth. If your cat becomes agitated, stop the process and continue another day.

Make sure you speak softly and soothingly throughout the entire process and do not forget to reward your cat with a yummy treat afterward. Be cautious not to overdo it the first few times or if your kitty becomes agitated. Take your time and increase the length of each session slowly.

If brushing your cat's teeth ends with tears, hurt feelings, or blood, there are still a few other choices you can make to improve her oral health. Dry kibble is better for your Siamese cat's teeth than soft or wet food, as soft food can become stuck between her teeth, causing tooth decay. There are also synthetic bones and chew toys that have been specifically designed to strengthen your cat's gums and teeth.

Never use human toothpaste or mouthwash for your Siamese cat, as it contains fluoride, which is toxic for cats. Look for a specially formulated toothpaste at your local pet store; often, they come in a variety of flavors such as beef, chicken, or salmon. There is also cat mouthwash that is diluted in water to kill bacteria and prevent plaque buildup.

Routine dental cleanings

No matter how disciplined you are about cleaning your Siamese cat's teeth, you will never really be able to give them a deep, thorough cleaning with just a toothbrush. Even if your pet has healthy teeth, it is wise to have your veterinarian give her an annual cleaning to remove any plaque and tartar buildup, clean the gum line, and polish her teeth.

Common Dental Issues in Siamese cats

No matter how often you brush your Siamese cat's teeth, you should inspect the inside of her mouth at least once a week. If you notice any of the following signs, take your cat to the vet as soon as possible:

- Bad breath
- Constantly pawing at her face or mouth
- A change of eating or chewing habits

Photo Courtesy of Jeremy Murray

- Depression
- Excessive drooling
- Red, swollen, painful, or bleeding gums
- Bumps or growths inside of the gum line
- Yellowish tartar buildup along the gum line
- Discolored, missing, or misaligned teeth

Feline dental care may be a hassle, but regular maintenance is a money saver in the long run and may even be a lifesaver. Letting your cat's teeth deteriorate leads to expensive and painful vet visits down the road. Many cats will need to be given anesthesia to have their teeth and gums cleaned.

Gingivitis – Gingivitis is caused by an accumulation of plaque, bacteria, and tartar around the gum. The signs are swollen, bleeding gums and extremely bad breath. Fortunately, it can easily be cleared up with regular brushing.

Mouth tumors – Mouth tumors look like small bumps or lumps on your cat's gums. They can be extremely painful and irritating for your cat while eating or drinking water. Mouth tumors will need to be surgically removed by a vet.

Periodontal disease – This gum infection results in tooth loss and a high risk of the infection spreading throughout the body, causing all sorts of maladies. Watch out for bad breath, nasal discharge, mouth pain, lack of appetite, and loose teeth.

Proliferating gum disease – This occurs when your cat's gumline is over her teeth, causing a gum infection. It can easily be treated with antibiotics.

Salivary cysts – These are fluid-filled blisters located under your cat's tongue or along the corners of her mouth. They will need to be professionally drained and cauterized. Often the salivary gland will need to be surgically removed.

Moral of the story: Keep your Siamese cat's teeth sparkling white, and you will both be smiling.

Ears

Your Siamese cat has a keen sense of hearing and can pick up the sound of a can of food being opened across the house, but her ears need a little help from you to stay clean. Monitoring your kitty's ears once a week for wax, debris, and infection will help those sensitive detectors stay alert to your every move.

Outer ear exam

A healthy feline ear flap has a layer of hair on the outer surface with no bald spots. The inner surface is clean and light pink. If you notice any discharge, redness, or swelling, your cat's ears should be checked by a veterinarian.

Inner ear exam

Place your kitty inside a quiet room with plenty of light and no other pets nearby. Gently fold back the ear and look inside. Healthy inner ears will be pale pink, have no debris or odor, and should have minimal earwax. If you find that your cat's ears are caked with wax, or you detect a foul odor, please consult with your vet as soon as possible.

Photo Courtesy of Carmen Medina

How to clean your Siamese cat's ears:

1. If your Siamese cat's ears appear to be dirty or waxy, use a small piece of gauze or a cotton ball dampened in mineral oil or a liquid ear cleaner formulated for cats.
2. Gently fold back your kitten's ear and carefully wipe away any ear wax or debris you can see.
3. Instead of rubbing the ear to remove the debris or ear wax, gently wipe it away. Do not attempt to clean the canal; probing inside of your cat's ear can cause trauma or infection.

Signs of ear problems:

- Brownish or yellowish discharge
- Sensitive to touch
- Red and swollen inner ear canal
- Hearing loss
- Excessive shaking of the head or tilting to the side
- Scabby skin around the ear flap
- Strong odor emanating from the ear
- Loss of balance
- Ear scratching or wiping ears on the floor or rubbing ears against the furniture

If you notice a brownish or black buildup of earwax (that looks like coffee grounds) in your Siamese cat's ear, she could have microscopic ear mites. Be sure to make an appointment with your vet as soon as possible.

Eyes

I have found that a waterless foam bath is the best mechanism for keeping your Siamese cat's coat at its best. Some cats love to be brushed and combed, but it is not a necessity. Make sure you keep those beautiful blue eyes clear of sleep crust. You never know when the next photo op will happen!

JULIE ZWEMKE
Zelines

A good home eye exam just before a brushing session can clue you into any tearing, crust, cloudiness, or inflammation that may be an indication of a health issue. Here are some simple suggestions to keep your kitty's eyes bright and healthy.

- Place your kitty in a brightly lit room and look into her eyes. They should be clear and bright, and the area around the eyeball should be white. Her pupils should be equal in size.
- Gently roll down your cat's eyelid with your thumb and check the inner lining. It should be pink, not white or red.
- Wipe away any crusty gunk from the corner of your cat's eyes with a damp cotton ball. Be sure to use a fresh cotton ball for each eye. Snip away any hairs that may be blocking her vision or poking her eyes.

The following symptoms are clear indications your Siamese cat may have an eye infection:

- Crusty gunk and discharge around the corners of the eyes
- Cloudiness
- Swollen eyelid
- Unequal pupil size
- No desire to open the eyes
- Teary eyes and tearstains

Keep the hair around your Siamese cat's eyes trimmed. Use a small pair of scissors, like cuticle scissors, to minimize the risk of injuring your cat. Long hair around the eyes can accidentally poke or scratch the pupils. Air conditioners will dry out your cat's eyes, causing irritation and possibly infection.

Professional Grooming

Grooming your Siamese cat may seem like an easy way to save money and bond with your kitty. But the grooming process is not for everyone, as it takes time, patience, and it is a whole lot trickier than it sounds. Thankfully, there is a stress-free option! Professional groomers have the skills and expertise to make sure your Siamese cat gets a trim and bath. After all, your furry friend deserves to be pampered.

Not all cats enjoy being handled by humans, which can make grooming a challenge. Sometimes you may require expert assistance if your cat has a temper or you simply feel uncomfortable with your grooming skills.

Professional groomers are trained to put even the feistiest kitty at ease while they get them clean.

There are pros and cons associated with taking your cat to a professional groomer. Here is the nitty-gritty:

ADVANTAGES

- Professional groomers have years of experience and can groom your cat in less time than you.
- Groomers use professional equipment and tools, ensuring a top-notch job.
- Groomers provide specialized treatments such as de-shedding and ringworm.
- They provide a quick medical exam, and upon request, they will pluck and clean your Siamese cat's ears.
- Most groomers include nail trimming.
- Many groomers will come to your house for an additional cost.

DISADVANTAGES

- The cost can add up, especially if your Siamese cat gets groomed frequently.
- Some Siamese cats suffer from anxiety and stress from being left alone at the groomer for two to three hours.
- Finding the perfect groomer for your Siamese cat takes time.
- Transporting your cat to and from the groomer may be troublesome if she does not enjoy long car rides.

In the end, the decision to use a professional groomer or not depends on your personal preference and situation. Ask yourself if you have the time and patience to groom your Siamese cat yourself or if you can financially afford to send her regularly to the groomer.

Many cat owners prefer combining both methods in order to save money, and in the meantime, they can gain experience grooming their cats themselves at home. For example, they may get their cat professionally groomed once every four to five months, and in between, they will do minor grooming touch-ups and baths.

Before you choose a groomer, take the time to research your options. Ask friends and colleagues for recommendations. Once you have narrowed down your options, be sure to ask the groomer the following questions. Feel free to ask any other questions that concern the well-being of your Siamese cat.

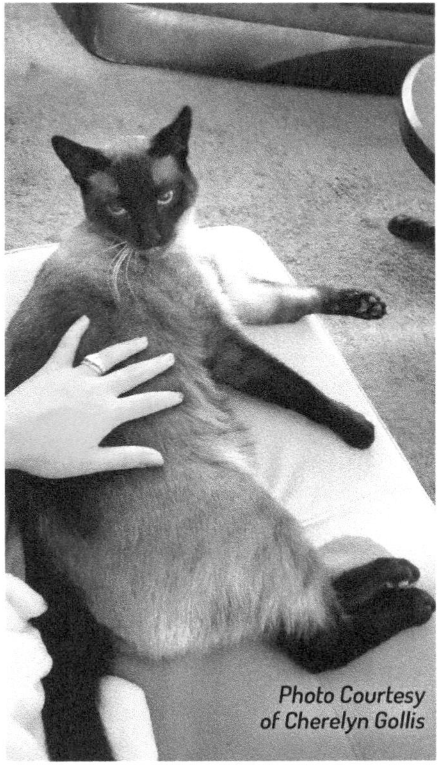
Photo Courtesy of Cherelyn Gollis

Can I see your facility?

The grooming facility should be clean, well-ventilated, and modern. The washtubs and tables should be sturdy. Ask yourself as you observe the facility if you feel comfortable leaving your furry companion there. If the groomer is standoffish and refuses to let you into the facility, move on to the next option on your list.

Do they have liability?

Any reputable groomer will have liability insurance, as it will be a registered business. Using a groomer with liability coverage will give you peace of mind if your Siamese cat has an unfortunate accident while in the groomer's care, as any medical expenses incurred will be covered.

What is the total cost?

Never assume that one groomer will charge the same as another. Always ask what services are included in basic grooming. Groomers often charge different fees depending on the cat's size, coat, and temperament. Often, groomers offer discounts for regular clients.

What type of training have they received?

Many groomers are self-trained. Be sure to look for a groomer who has been professionally trained through an apprenticeship, etc. Ask groomers how long they have been professionally grooming cats and if they have experience grooming Siamese cats.

CHAPTER 11

Preventative Medical Care

> *Regular visits to a Vet are a good idea, especially as your Siamese gets older. Remember cats are not 'Complainers' when it comes to health and it is oftentimes difficult to tell when your Siamese is not feeling well. Visits to your Vet will help to make sure your Siamese stays health as they grow older.*
>
> WILLIAM HARRISON
> *Kittentanz Cattery*

By making your Siamese cat's health a priority, you will avoid a long list of medical issues and increase the overall well-being of your furry friend. Get the facts about preventative care, vaccines, parasites, and alternative medical treatments to enhance your cat's quality of life.

Choosing a Veterinarian

Choosing the right veterinarian for your Siamese cat is something you should carefully consider, as this person needs to keep your cat healthy and may even save her life. Both you and your kitten should agree about this person before making a commitment to work with him or her.

Before you start checking out different veterinary clinics in your region, make a list of your priorities for your Siamese cat. This will help you narrow down your options when choosing a vet and help you ask the right questions. Consider your cat's age, family history (if known), and any health concerns. For example, if your furry friend is getting older, look for a vet who specializes in geriatric feline care.

Here is a basic checklist of essential requirements for veterinarians (requirements may vary depending on your cat's needs):

- Proximity to your house – If there is an emergency, can you get to the veterinary clinic quickly?
- Pricing – Every veterinary clinic has different prices; make sure the clinic you choose fits your budget.
- Do the clinic's hours work with your work schedule, or will you need to take time off to take your Siamese cat there?
- Does the clinic have up-to-date facilities with cutting-edge medical technology and care?

Photo Courtesy of Becky Brown

- Check for generous appointment times, as you do not want to feel rushed during the visit.
- A smaller practice means you most likely will see the same vet every time you visit, plus your Siamese cat can develop a rapport with the medical staff.
- Does the staff have knowledge of alternative and holistic treatments?
- Is the staff involved in the local animal welfare community, such as pet rescue organizations?

Once you have narrowed down what you want from a veterinarian, it is time to start your search for potential candidates.

Ask for personal recommendations – The best place to start is word of mouth. Ask fellow cat owners whose pet-care philosophies are in line with your own about their vets. Or ask a friend or family member for recommendations. Many veterinarian clinics offer a referral program, which may mean discounts for you and the friend who referred you.

Look for licensed personnel – Be sure to check out the American Animal Hospital Association (AAHA) website. There you will find an extensive list of accredited veterinarians in your region, as well as an evaluation of the facility, staff, patient care, and equipment. This is a great option if you have just moved to a new area and do not know who to ask.

Whether you get a referral from a friend or from an online search, make sure the veterinarian clinic is accredited with the AAHA. The AAHA regularly evaluates veterinary practices throughout the United States on their standards for patient care, pain management, facilities, surgery, medical records, cleanliness, anesthesiology, and more. While veterinary clinics are not required to be accredited by law, accreditation shows you a clinic is committed to maintaining only the highest standard of care or service.

Find a veterinary clinic that specializes in cats – Not all veterinarians are created equal. Some veterinarians specialize in livestock, such as cows, goats, horses, etc. If you live in a rural area, be sure to verify that the veterinarian has expertise in treating cats specifically; ask how much experience they have with felines before making an appointment.

Ask for a tour of the veterinary clinic – When you narrow the list down to one or two veterinary practices, ask to take a tour of the facility. Any reputable vet will be more than happy to show you around the clinic and make you feel comfortable. Notice whether the staff is caring, calm, and courteous. Another important aspect to observe is the cleanliness of the lobby, waiting rooms, and exam rooms.

In addition to getting a feel for the facility, ask plenty of questions. Vets appreciate when pet owners are interested in their pets' health and well-being.

Here are some questions you should ask when interviewing the vet:

- How are overnight patients monitored?
- Are all diagnostic tests, like bloodwork, ultrasounds, X-rays, etc., done on-site or in another location?
- Are all veterinary technicians employed by the clinic licensed by the state to practice on animals?
- Does the facility refer patients to specialists if needed? (Their answer should be affirmative.)
- What types of payment plans does the practice accept? Are there special payment plans for major surgeries or treatments?

The questions above are simply guidelines. Feel free to ask any other questions that concern you and your Siamese cats.

Once you have decided on a vet, be a good client. Show up early for appointments to fill out any necessary paperwork. Be patient and understanding if you have to wait longer than expected. Your vet sometimes has to attend to emergencies, which take precedence over routine appointments.

Photo Courtesy of Autumn Tucker

Be prepared to be your Siamese cat's advocate, but know when it is time to step back and let your vet take over.

If you or your cat do not feel comfortable with the vet, do not hesitate to switch facilities. Veterinary clinics expect clients to come and go. However, before your departure, be sure to request a complete copy of your Siamese cat's medical file. You can ask that your cat's health records be faxed or mailed to either you or the new clinic.

Microchipping

Each year, more than eight million pets end up in a shelter across the country, and fewer than 20 percent are reclaimed.

A microchip is about the size of a grain of rice. It is implanted in the loose skin between your Siamese cat's shoulder blades, and your cat will not even notice it is there. It is no more invasive than a vaccination. Getting your cat microchipped costs around $30 to $50, depending on your vet.

The microchip itself does not have a battery; it is activated by a scanner that is passed over the location where the chip was implanted. The radio waves put out by the scanner activate the chip. The chip sends the scanner an identification number, which appears on the screen. The microchip is not a GPS device and cannot track your cat if she gets lost.

If your Siamese cat is found and taken to a veterinary clinic or shelter, one of the first things they will do is scan her for a microchip. Once they find the microchip registry information, they will quickly locate you to be reunited with your cat. Make sure to keep your cat's microchip data up to date with your personal information.

Another advantage to microchipping is if your cat is ever stolen, the thief will most likely remove your cat's collar and ID tags and toss them in the trash. Often, the thief will resell the cat to an unknown victim. With a microchip, you can prove the cat is yours.

Generally, the entire microchipping process takes only a few seconds, or about the time it takes to give your cat an injection. It will take more time for you to fill out all of the paperwork involved than it will to insert the microchip! Microchipping does not necessarily have to be completed by a vet, but it is highly recommended if you use a vet's service.

If your kitty is squeamish around injections and needles, you might want to consider getting her chipped at the same time she is being neutered. Most pet owners opt to have their feline friends chipped when they are spayed or neutered for this very reason. The pain is similar to using a needle to draw blood; some cats flinch, and others do not.

Pet doors can be programmed to recognize your cat's microchip, letting her come into the house but keeping other animals outside.

Photo Courtesy of Ines Alonso

Once your Siamese cat is microchipped, there are two things you need to do each year. First, ask your veterinarian to scan your cat's microchip at least once a year to make sure it is still working and can be detected. Second, keep your online registration information up to date. It only takes a few minutes to check the information, and you can rest easy that you have improved your chances of getting your Siamese cat back if the unexpected should happen.

Neutering and Spaying

There are numerous reasons to spay or neuter your Siamese cat. Neutering or spaying simplifylies pet ownership, as it prevents females from going into heat and, according to some experts, improves feline behavior.

Many Siamese cat owners get their cats spayed or neutered to comply with the breeder's contract. However, other cat owners opt to leave their cat's anatomy intact for personal reasons or because they plan on using their Siamese cats as show cats. However, be aware that this presents occasional challenges. For example, your intact cat may be barred from some boarding kennels.

Spaying and neutering have some direct health benefits for your Siamese cat. Testicular and ovarian cancers are nonexistent, and there is evidence that spaying reduces the risk of mammary cancer and uterine infections. Another benefit is that fixed cats live longer than intact cats.

Traditionally, male or female cats were neutered at six months of age, but this is after many cats reach sexual maturity and not based on any scientific rationale. For social, health, and population control reasons, it is preferable and recommended to get your cat spayed or neutered at four months of age.

In the past, it was suggested that all female cats should be allowed to have at least one litter of kittens. However, this is totally unnecessary and provides no benefit whatsoever to the cat. It is, therefore, preferable to have a female cat spayed before she reaches sexual maturity (about four months of age).

Once your female cat reaches sexual maturity, she will come into season or "call." Sexual cycles occur every three to four weeks in Siamese cats, and it can be quite a noisy affair, as the name applies. There are drugs that can suppress the sexual cycle, but they have a long list of side effects in cats and are not recommended for long-term use. If you are not planning to breed your Siamese cat, having her spayed will eliminate this undesirable sexual behavior.

Spaying is a simple surgical procedure performed by a qualified veterinarian. The procedure involves removing your female cat's ovaries and uterus. Here are a few reasons why you should consider spaying your Siamese cat:

- Spaying reduces the risk of urinary tract infections and breast cancer. It is highly recommended you spay your Siamese cat before her first heat to prevent health complications in the future.
- Spaying reduces unwanted pregnancies, which saves you from unplanned expenses.
- A spayed cat will not go into heat. A female cat in heat will urinate all over the house and yowl loudly while trying to attract a mate.

Neutering is a simple procedure performed by a qualified veterinarian, which involves removing your male cat's testicles. Here are a few reasons why you should consider neutering your Siamese cat:

- Neutering prevents testicular cancer.
- Your Siamese cat will not roam about the neighborhood in search of a mate. An unneutered male cat will do everything in his power to find a mate, including digging a hole under the fence or running across a busy highway.
- A neutered cat will be less aggressive and better behaved than an unneutered cat. Also, he will not have the desire to mark his territory by spraying urine everywhere.

Many concerns you may have about getting your Siamese cat spayed or neutered are just misinformation. Consider the following:

Will your cat feel remorse or loss? No. Cats do not suffer from emotional insecurities or experience societal pressures to have a family as human do. They do not need to procreate to feel emotionally fulfilled.

Does spaying or neutering cause obesity? Contrary to popular opinion, spaying and neutering will not make your Siamese cat fat. However, a lack of exercise and overfeeding will.

Are there negative side effects? As with all surgical procedures, there are certain risks, but these are minor and rare and often occur when the procedure is not performed by a reputable veterinarian.

As mentioned earlier in this book, Siamese cats' hair color is determined by temperature. So, when a patch of hair is shaved off for an operation such as spaying, the new hair may grow back a darker color. However, this is only temporary, and as further hair growth occurs, the dark hair will be replaced by normal lighter hair.

Many states and counties have established low-cost programs for spaying or neutering, which makes these types of surgeries an affordable option for all pet owners. The web page for the Humane Society will provide you with a list of local, affordable clinics and funding options to help you cover the cost of the procedure. If you are not planning on professionally breeding your Siamese cat, then you should definitely consider getting your Siamese cat neutered or spayed.

Internal Parasites

Even though you may do everything possible to protect your cat, she may be affected by parasites at some point in her life. These microscopic organisms carry disease and can cause serious health issues in your four-legged family member if not treated quickly. Some parasites can be passed to your cat from contaminated soil or other cat's stool, and certain types of worms may even infect humans.

There are five main types of worms that commonly affect Siamese cats: hookworms, whipworms, roundworms, and tapeworms. Heartworm disease is uncommon in cats but increasing in incidence, especially in southern parts of North America. Most internal parasites in cats are usually ingested and affect the cat's gastrointestinal tract.

By familiarizing yourself with these common parasites, you will learn how to keep your cat safe. While each parasite affects cats differently, there are some general warning signs that your Siamese cat may have parasites:

- Abdominal pain
- Vomiting
- Diarrhea that lasts longer than 24 hours
- Unexplained weight loss
- Pot-bellied appearance
- Extreme lethargy
- Dehydration
- Poor coat appearance, hair loss, or hot spots
- Coughing

Roundworms

If a kitten is infected with a large number of roundworms, the worms can stunt the kitten's growth, cause serious digestive upset, and cause the kitten to become anemic, resulting in excessive gas formation. Often these kittens have a characteristic "pot-bellied" appearance.

Roundworms are one of the most common types of internal parasite in cats and can be transmitted to humans. Many kittens are born with roundworms as they are passed on from their mother. Roundworms can be diagnosed by your vet with a small fecal sample, and they are treated with deworming medications.

Hookworms

Hookworms can be fatal in kittens if left untreated. There are several types of hookworms that attach themselves to the cat's intestinal wall to gorge themselves on blood, causing anemia. Your cat can get hookworms from ingesting contaminated fecal matter, or the parasite can be passed on to kittens through their mother's milk. Humans can become infected with hookworms. Treatment involves a deworming medication, which will need to be administered twice.

Tapeworms

Tapeworms require an intermediate host, such as a flea, a bird, or a rodent, in order to complete their life cycle. In other words, your cat cannot get tapeworm from coming into contact with an infected dog or cat. Cats most often get tapeworms from eating an infected flea. When a cat consumes a flea that is infested with tapeworm eggs, the egg will attach itself to the cat's intestines and hatch. Infected cats may scoot their rear end on the ground.

Often, pieces of the tapeworm may break off and resemble small pieces of rice in an infected cat's stool.

If you suspect your Siamese cat has tapeworms, take a stool sample to your vet for diagnosis. Treatment involves a combination of oral medicine, injections, and fumigating your houses for fleas.

Heartworms

Heartworm is uncommon in cats, but cases are increasing in southern states. Heartworms are spread by mosquitoes; a mosquito, when feeding on a cat, may inject heartworm larvae into the bloodstream. These larvae mature and ultimately travel to the heart, taking up residence in major blood vessels of the heart and lungs.

Heartworm symptoms may vary from cat to cat. Heartworm disease may cause coughing, rapid breathing, unexplained weight loss, and vomiting. Occasionally, a cat that is infected will die suddenly, and the diagnosis will be discovered in a post-mortem examination. Heartworms are large and can reach 6 to 15 inches in length.

The best approach to heartworms is prevention, as treating heartworms is extremely expensive and can have serious side effects. Also, treating heartworms requires keeping your cat confined without exercise for long periods of time in order to prevent heart damage. Even if your cat is regularly taking heartworm preventatives, she will need to be tested regularly for worms.

How can I prevent or treat these parasites?

Speak to your veterinarian about the most appropriate parasite control program for your Siamese cat. Prompt treatment should be given when any intestinal parasites are detected.

However, the majority of internal parasites will need to be diagnosed by your veterinarian via a microscopic examination of your cat's stool. If you notice any of the symptoms mentioned above, your vet will ask you to bring in a small sample of your cat's stool. Even if your cat is not exhibiting any symptoms, it is highly recommended you take a cat stool sample with you to your Siamese cat's annual check-up.

Your vet will set up a regular deworming schedule for your Siamese cat to treat different types of intestinal parasites, as well as prevent heartworms. The bottom line is prevention, flea control, and regular testing are the best actions to prevent consequences caused by internal parasites.

Fleas and Ticks

Your Siamese cat's soft, warm fur provides the ideal environment for fleas and ticks. These disgusting bugs feed on your cat's blood and may cause a long list of problems, such as allergic reactions and serious illnesses caused by a tick bite. Even though fleas and ticks are more prevalent during the warmer months, you will still need to ward them off during the colder months.

Fleas

These pesky insects not only set up home on your cat but will quickly invade your home. They have the ability to jump almost three feet and can survive in the harshest environments. The average life span for a flea can be 12 days to an entire year. During this time, a single flea can produce millions of baby fleas.

If not controlled, fleas can cause serious health complications for their host. For example, a flea can consume approximately 15 times its body weight in blood each day, causing your Siamese cat to become anemic. Some cats have an allergic reaction to flea bites, which is called allergic dermatitis.

Flea warning signs:

- Hair loss
- Allergic dermatitis
- Flea eggs look like white grains of sand

Photo Courtesy of Susie Kelley

- Flea droppings look like tiny dirt particles
- Excessive biting, licking, or scratching
- Hot spots or scabs

Flea droppings can be found throughout your Siamese cat's coat. Use a fine-toothed comb to detect them, especially around your cat's abdomen, ears, mouth, and tail.

Fleas are expert stowaways. They quickly attach themselves to animals while outside or can jump from one cat to another. Even if your cat never goes outside, she can still get fleas that have attached themselves to you. If not controlled, fleas can invade your house within a day or two.

If your Siamese has fleas, all of your resident pets will need to be treated. In some extreme cases, the inside of your house will need to be fumigated. Your veterinarian will confirm your suspicions and most likely will suggest one or two of the following treatments:

- Oral or topical treatment or cat-formulated shampoo for your Siamese cat.
- Thoroughly cleaning your house, including bedding, rugs, and upholstery. A severe infestation will require professional help, which means you and all your pets will have to temporarily evacuate your home.

How to prevent fleas:

- Wash your Siamese cat's bedding regularly in hot, soapy water, and brush her using a flea brush.
- There are preventive flea-control measures available either by prescription or over the counter. Be aware some flea collars can be carcinogenic for animals and humans. Always consult with your vet beforehand.

Ticks

Ticks are considered parasites as they feed on the host's blood. Ticks are experts at concealing themselves by burrowing into their hosts and then gorging on their blood. They can transmit serious diseases to both animals and humans. Transmission varies in certain areas and climates. Ask your vet what types of ticks are in your locality.

If your Siamese cat goes outside, she will be an easy target for ticks. You will need to be alert year-round, but be extra vigilant during late spring and early summer.

How to check your Siamese cat for ticks:

Ticks are very small, making them very easy to miss until they bite your cat and begin to swell up with all the blood they have sucked. Carefully run your fingers through your Siamese cat's coat, paying extra attention to warm spots such as the inside of her ears and around her feet and face. Be sure to repeat this every time any of your pets come inside from playing.

Health complications caused by tick bites:

- Blood loss and anemia
- Tick paralysis
- Allergic dermatitis

If you find a tick attached to your Siamese cat, it is essential you carefully remove it, as the tick's blood may infect you or your cat. Humans may contract Lyme Disease from deer ticks; these ticks are the primary carrier of Lyme Disease. The illness causes depression, fever, loss of appetite, painful joints, and kidney failure. Lyme disease needs to be caught in time to be successfully treated with antibiotics.

Follow these instructions to safely remove a tick:

1. Prepare a glass jar with rubbing alcohol inside. This allows you to take a tick in for testing at your veterinary clinic. Put on latex gloves and ask a family member to distract your Siamese cat while you extract the tick.

2. Using a pair of disinfected tweezers, gently grasp the tick as close as you can to the cat's skin. Pull straight upward, using even pressure, then place the tick into the jar with rubbing alcohol. Do not twist the tick out, as this could leave the head attached inside the cat or cause the tick to regurgitate infected fluids.

3. Disinfect the bitten area and the tweezers; wash your hands with warm, soapy water afterward. Monitor the area for the next few weeks for any signs of an infection. If there is a sign of infection, take your Siamese cat and the tick to the veterinarian for a check-up.

Many products used to treat or prevent fleas are also useful in killing ticks. Keep your yard tick-free by keeping the grass cut and by removing any large weeds that could be hiding places for ticks.

Holistic Alternatives to Conventional Veterinary Medicine

Holistic veterinary care is often combined with conventional medicine to aid a cat's healing process. For example, if your Siamese cat has a hip or knee replacement, she will need to take medications such as antibiotics to prevent infection. But some veterinarians recommend combining the treatment with holistic care such as acupuncture or massages to naturally ease the pain and hasten the healing process.

Below are some of the most popular holistic treatments recommended by veterinarians and used by concerned pet parents. Be aware that few of these treatments have been scientifically proven in treating felines. Before starting any type of holistic treatment, be sure to talk over the risks and details with your veterinarian.

Feline acupuncture

Acupuncture uses needles to stimulate pressure points to release the buildup of certain chemicals in the muscles, spinal cord, and brain, thus promoting better health. There is plenty of anecdotal proof that acupuncture can relieve cats of joint and muscle pain, encourage healing post-surgery, and even treat cancer or other types of traumas.

Chinese herbal medicine

Chinese herbal medicine combines certain herbs to relieve pain, improve and restore organ function, and strengthen the immune system. Many pet owners rave about Chinese herbal medicine's effect on their pets. As with all herbs, make sure they are safe to use alongside your cat's conventional medications, such as blood thinners or diuretics.

Magnetic field therapy

According to the Veterinary Clinics of America, magnet therapy is gaining popularity in the United States to treat illness and injury; however, there is not much evidence that the application of magnets can heal your Siamese cat. Magnet field therapy is affordable, non-invasive, and has virtually no side effects.

Feline massage

Feline massage encourages healing, improves circulation, stimulates nerves, relieves stress, and relaxes your cat's muscles. One of the biggest advantages of a kitty massage is that it makes your feline friend feel good and strengthens the bond between a person and the cat. Massage will not cure your Siamese cat's cancer or injury; it will, however, make her feel relaxed and loved.

Nutritional supplements

Nutritional supplements are required if you are feeding your cat a homemade diet to make up for any nutritional deficiencies. Look for nutritional supplements that include calcium, omega fatty acids, vitamins, and amino acids.

Photo Courtesy of Shawn Quinet

When choosing a holistic treatment or supplement for your cat, be sure to use good judgment and always consult with your veterinarian to see if the treatment will help your furry friend. Note: just because an herbal substance claims it is healthy and beneficial does not mean that it is harmless. Always thoroughly research a product before giving it to your cat.

Vaccinations

Even if your Siamese cat stays inside all of the time, she will still need to be updated with her vaccinations. Your cat can catch an airborne virus or germs that comes through the window or door. And even the most docile felines sometimes make a run for it. If your cat accidentally gets outside, you want to be sure she is protected. Indoor cats may also pick up viruses when they stay at a kennel or if you bring home a new pet.

Despite common belief, your Siamese cat does not have nine lives, so you need to protect her. The right vaccinations will protect your kitty from diseases caused by viruses and bacteria.

Your vet can help you figure out what vaccines are best and how often your kitty should get her vaccines. It often will depend on your feline's age, overall health, and lifestyle. Your vet also knows how long each vaccine is effective and will take into consideration how likely your cat is to come into contact with a certain disease. Many local and state governments have requirements regarding rabies.

When to give vaccines: Kittens should start to receive a series of vaccinations when they are about six to eight weeks old until they are about sixteen weeks old. Then, they will require a booster shot when they are a year old. Adult cats typically require vaccines every year or every second year, depending on how long each vaccine is designed for.

Here are some of the most recommended vaccines for cats:

- Rabies
- Panleukopenia (also known as feline distemper)
- Feline calicivirus
- Feline viral rhinotracheitis

The feline viral rhinotracheitis, calicivirus, and panleukopenia vaccine often comes as a combination shot and is referred to as a "distemper shot."

Your cat may require additional shots depending on how often she is outside and is in contact with other pets and diseases that are common in your area. Such diseases include:

Feline leukemia – This is a serious infection that spreads through bodily fluids, such as saliva, feces, urine, and milk. This vaccine is highly recommended for kittens. Feline leukemia cannot be cured, so prevention is the key.

Bordetella – Often referred to as kennel cough. Cats who frequently go to the groomer or stay at a kennel should be vaccinated against this infection, as it spreads quickly in spaces with lots of animals. The vaccine will not prevent the disease but will prevent your feline friend from getting very sick and passing it on to other pets.

Administering Medicine

Being ill is no fun, especially when you have to take medicine. For your furry friends, it is no different.

Here are a few useful tips on how to make the process of giving your cat medicine less stressful for both you and her.

Holding your cat

Some cats simply do not enjoy being held. If this is the case with your cat, approach her carefully, speaking in a calm, gentle voice as you scoop her up. Wrap your cat up in a towel or blanket, fully supporting her legs so that they are not dangling, which can make her feel unsure and uncomfortable.

How to give your cat a pill

Most medicine for cats comes in the form of capsules or pills. Have the specified medicine already in your hand. Keep in mind that Siamese cats are extremely intelligent cats, and do not take kindly to changes in their routine, so most likely, they will not make it easy on you. Unlike a dog who will happily scarf down a pill camouflaged in a spoonful of peanut butter, you will need to approach your cat in a calm but calculated way.

If your cat tends to be cooperative, you can attempt to put the pill directly into her mouth. Avoid tossing the pill into her mouth, as she will most likely spit it right back out. Instead, place the pill on the center of her tongue, near the back of her mouth, then gently rub her throat to encourage the pill to go down. After this, offer your kitty a bowl of fresh water to help wash the medicine down.

Some cats require a stealthier move than simply placing medicine in their mouth. Try concealing the pill in your cat's usual food dish with her usual food; wet or semi-moist food works the best. If your furry friend only eats dry kibble, you can give her moist food instead for an exciting treat when you give her medicine.

Another method is to hide the medicine in a small ball of food. Your cat will be able to play with the ball of food with the hidden medicine inside, and eventually, she will eat it without realizing it. The only problem with this method is it tends to be quite messy.

Avoid the temptation to conceal your cat's medicine in human food. Many foods can cause gastrointestinal distress in cats, even more so if your cat is already feeling under the weather. Always check with your veterinarian before giving your cat non-pet foods when she is ill.

Never grind or crush your cat's medicine into a powder form unless your vet recommends it. Crushed medicine tends to taste bitter, and your cat will often spit it up after eating, so she will not get her full dosage.

If your vet recommends crushing your cat's medicine to administer it, try to crush the pill between two spoons or consider investing in a pill crusher from your local pharmacy. This tool makes crushing pills a little less messy and easier, as the medication is confined to the device.

Stir the crushed-up medicine in a small portion of cat food gravy. The strong gravy flavor will mellow the gross flavor of the medicine. Never give your cat her medicine in milk, as most Siamese cats are lactose intolerant. If she refuses a spoonful of gravy, incorporate it into her regular food as a special topping for kibble or mixed into her wet food.

LIQUID FORMULA

Sometimes a vet will prescribe a liquid formula of your cat's medicine to be administered via syringe when your cat refuses to take her medicine or she cannot eat normally. Most liquid medications need to be kept in the refrigerator; however, cats, in general, are more likely to accept the liquid formula at room temperature. Never warm up the formula in the microwave. Warm it up by holding the syringe in your hands for a few minutes.

As mentioned above, you will need to hold your cat in a comfortable position with the syringe in your dominant hand. Allow your kitty to lick the tip of the syringe so she can taste the medicine, then slowly depress the plunger. Try to aim the stream of liquid directly toward the back of your cat's throat, being careful not to tilt her head back, as this may cause her to choke.

Once the liquid formula is in your cat's mouth, try to hold her mouth closed to make sure she swallows the liquid. There is no need to worry if your furry friend tries to spit some of it up, as that is very typical behavior for cats. Avoid re-medicating your Siamese and wait for the next dosage.

EYE AND EAR DROPS

Sometimes a cat may need to take eye or ear drops, particularly if she suffers from allergies. Just as when you administer pills or liquid medications, you will need to securely hold your cat so that she does not squirm or jump away.

For eye drops, place one of your hands on top of the cat's head. Using two of your fingers, gently pull back the upper eyelid. Place your remaining fingers under your kitty's jaw to support her head. Using your other hand, use an eye dropper to drop in the specified dose. Never touch your cat's eyes with the eyedropper or with your fingers.

HEALTH ALERT!
Eye Troubles?

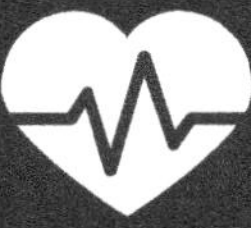

Siamese cats have a reputation for being more likely to be cross-eyed, but what causes this? This cross-eyed appearance, also known as strabismus, doesn't cause any visual impairment in many cases. However, the retinas of these Siamese cats are shifted, so to see straight, the cat needs to turn its eyes slightly inward to line up with the retinas, giving the cross-eyed appearance. The genetic trait that causes strabismus is also tied to the cat's coloration.

For eye drops, gently massage the base of your cat's ear in a circular motion. You should hear a squishing noise as the medication penetrates the ear canal. Unfortunately, your cat will not like either of these methods, but there's no avoiding it if she needs ear medicine.

INJECTIONS

Certain illnesses, such as diabetes, will require you to inject a tiny dosage under your cat's skin. A second set of hands can help keep your fur baby in place while you administer the medication.

Your cat may require an injection in her hip, neck, or other site, depending on the medication and veterinarian's instructions. Your vet will show you how and where you should give the injection. The vet will explain whether the injection should go into a muscle, vein, or a fold in the skin. Always use a new needle for each injection. After each injection, be sure to give your furry friend some extra cuddles and attention.

Never throw the needle in the garbage when you are finished. Instead, dispose of it in an approved container for sharp items.

You should never give your Siamese cat over-the-counter medicines formulated for people, including eye drops because these medicines can be hazardous. Instead, if you suspect your cat is sick, contact your vet to schedule a check-up and only give your cat the specific medicine prescribed by your cat's doctor.

Pet Insurance

No matter how careful you are with your Siamese cat, unexpected accidents do happen, and often they are not cheap.

Veterinary costs are higher than ever. According to the American Pet Product Association, an average cat owner spends almost $200 for annual check-ups. What happens when the unexpected occurs? Costs can quickly add up! For example, for an active cat such as a Siamese cat, the cost to repair a cruciate ligament tear in the knee (which often happens when the cat comes to a sudden stop while chasing something) was about $1,200 five years ago. Today, it can cost a whopping $5,000 for each knee.

Pet insurance can help defray these costs. Pet insurance was once a specialty niche, but in the last few years, it has gone mainstream. Currently, there are more than 15 different insurance companies in the United States that offer pet insurance, but less than 1 percent of cat owners purchase it.

Just as you can pick a health plan that matches you and your family's needs, you can also choose an insurance plan that is the best fit for your Siamese cat. Most insurance companies offer three types of coverage: accident and illness, accident only, and a wellness plan. Wellness plans often cover preventative care, such as annual check-ups and routine vaccinations. You can purchase one type of plan or add on an accident or illness policy.

The final price of pet insurance depends on your Siamese cat's age and the type of coverage you choose. You can expect to pay a monthly premium of about $20 to $50 a month. The deductible depends on the type of policy you choose.

Here are a few benefits and drawbacks of pet insurance:

- It gives you peace of mind knowing you have the resources for any unforeseen medical costs if your Siamese cat becomes injured or ill.
- Pet insurance gives vets the opportunity to give your kitty top-notch care without having to worry about incurring too many medical costs.
- Pet insurance helps your cat live a longer and healthier life, as you will not hesitate to take your cat in for medical treatment before her condition worsens.

- Some insurance companies look at factors such as the cat's age, whether she is purebred, and the cat's living environment. Depending on these factors, the monthly insurance premium could increase.
- Many insurance companies have a 48-hour waiting period before approving accident insurance and a 14-day waiting period before approval for illness insurance.
- Depending on the fine print of the insurance plan, it may exclude pre-existing illnesses, pregnancy and/or birth, routine vaccines, and dental maintenance.
- The majority of cat insurance plans require that you pay for the entire veterinary cost upfront and, afterward, submit a claim for reimbursement.

Note: Your pet insurance will be void if your Siamese cat is not up to date on her vaccinations and deworming. Also, if your cat gets sick from something that is preventable by being vaccinated, most insurance companies will not cover the expenses.

CONSIDER SELF-INSURING

If you decide that pet insurance is too expensive for your monthly budget, then another practical option is to set up a personal savings account for your Siamese cat. You can always deposit a certain amount of money in the account each month and only withdraw from it for your cat's medical care. This is an excellent option if you are disciplined with money.

The bottom line is veterinary care is not cheap, and it can quickly add up, especially if your Siamese cat needs expensive diagnostics, care, and treatment. If you do decide to purchase pet insurance, take your time and read the fine print very carefully to make sure you completely understand what you are getting yourself into.

CHAPTER 12

Showing Your Siamese Cat

Does your Siamese cat have what it takes to compete in a cat show? Knowing how to prepare and show your cat are some of the first steps to training a champion.

If your Siamese cat is extremely shy or easily frightened, then a cat show may not be the best choice. On the other hand, if your cat fares well with new people, noisy crowds, and being close to other cats, you might have a chance of winning the prize.

CFA Breeding Standards

The Cat Fanciers' Association (CFA) recognizes forty-five pedigreed breeds, as well as non-pedigreed breeds classed as Companion Cats. The forty-five pedigree breeds are eligible to compete in Championship, Premiership, Kitten, and Veteran Classes. Companion Cats are eligible to complete in the Household Pet class.

The CFA recognized the Siamese breed in 1906, the same year the CFA was founded. The Siamese breed standard was established in 1966 by Jeanne Singer and has remained unchanged since that date.

GENERAL APPEARANCE: The ideal Siamese cat should be medium-sized, svelte, with a long, refined silhouette, very lithe but muscular. Males may be slightly larger than female felines. Balance and refinement are essential to the breed, with neither too much nor too little attention given to any one of the cat's features.

HEAD: The Siamese cat's head should be long and taper into a wedge shape from the ears, forming a triangle. The head should be medium size in proportion to the body. The width should be the same between the eyes and ears. Allowance will be made for a stud cat.

SKULL: The skull should be flat. In profile, a long straight line should easily be noted from the top of the head to the tip of the nose. There should be no bulge over the eyes and no dip in the nose.

EARS: The feline's ears should be slightly oversized and pointed with a wide base.

NOSE: The nose should be long and straight, a natural extension of the forehead with no bulge or break.

MUZZLE: The feline should have a fine, wedge-shaped muzzle.

HISTORICAL FACT

Champion Wankee

Wankee was one of the foundational ancestors of the modern Siamese cat breed. Born on September 28, 1895, in Hong Kong, Wankee was imported to the United Kingdom in March 1896 by Mrs. Robinson in West Kensington. Mrs. Robinson was a member of the National Cat Club Committee and served as a judge for Siamese cats for that organization. Though Wankee was the first Siamese cat to become a show champion in the UK, his appearance was very different from the modern Siamese cat, including a larger build and less angular face.

EYES: The Siamese cat's eyes should be almond-shaped, medium-sized, neither protruding nor recessed and slanted toward the nose in harmony with the wedge shape of the head and ears. A feline will be disqualified if it has crossed eyes.

CHIN and JAW: The chin and jaw should be medium-sized. The tip of the chin must line up perfectly with the tip of the nose in the same vertical plane.

NECK: The neck should be long and slender.

LEGS: The feline's legs should be long and slim. The hind legs will be higher in the front, in proper proportion to the body.

PAWS: The Siamese cat should have dainty, small, and oval-shaped paws. There should be five toes in the front and four behind.

TAIL: The Siamese cat must have a long, thin tail that tapers to a fine point at the tip.

COAT: The coat must be short, fine textured, and glossy, lying against the feline's body.

CONDITION: The cat must be in excellent physical condition. Eyes must be clear and bright. The feline should be muscular, strong, and lithe. It should be neither flabby, nor bony, nor fat. A cat with a fat or mushy body may be penalized or disqualified.

BODY: The feline's body should have subtle shading according to color-point coding specified below. The CFA makes allowances for a darker color in older cats as Siamese cats, generally darken with age, but there must be a definite contrast between the color of the body and points. Points refer to the color tone on the mask, ears, legs, feet, and tail. All points should be the same shade. The mask should not extend over the top of the cat's head, with no tickling or white hairs in the points.

Currently, the CFA is the only cat registry dedicated to preserving and promoting the traditional four colors of the Siamese breed.

SEAL POINT: The body should be an even pale fawn or cream tone, with gradual shading to a lighter color on stomach and the chest. Points must be a deep seal brown. The nose and paw pads should be the same color as the points. Eye color should be a deep, vivid blue.

CHOCOLATE POINT: The cat's body should be an ivory tone, with little to no shading. Points should be a milk-chocolate tone. The nose and paw pads should be the same color as the points. Eye color should be a deep, vivid blue.

BLUE POINT: The body should be a bluish-white in tone with gradual shading to a white color on the stomach and chest. Points should be deep blue. The nose and paw pads should be a slate color. Eye color should be a deep, vivid blue.

LILAC POINT: The body should be glacial-white with no shading. Points should be frosty gray with a slight pinkish tone. The nose and paw pads should be lavender pink. Eyes a deep, vivid blue.

The CFA will disqualify any cats with evidence of illness or poor health, such as weak hind legs, mouth breathing due to a nasal obstruction, emaciation, or a visible kink in the tail. Also, a cat will be disqualified if it has eyes other than a deeply vivid blue color, has white toes or feet, has an incorrect number of toes, or has long hair.

The CFA disqualifies felines that have been declawed or that have received a tendonectomy surgery, as claws are essential for a cat's healthy, joyful life. Cats must be intact (not neutered or spayed) in order to be qualified as show cats.

The CFA rules stipulate that to be eligible for registration, a purebred Siamese cat must present an eight-generation pedigree that consists only of registered Siamese ancestors. In other words, the feline's parents and grandparents must have been registered as purebreds with the CFA.

The Thai Cat — TICA Standards

The International Cat Association (TICA) is considered one of the world's largest genetic registries of pedigreed and domestic cats. It is the only registry in the world to allow household cats of unknown ancestry to compete for the same titles and awards as pedigreed cats. TICA encourages knowledgeable breeding of pedigreed cats to preserve the distinct characteristics and traits of individual felines for future generations.

TICA currently recognizes seventy-one breeds of cats, including the Thai breed, which is considered to be the Old-Style Siamese. This

Photo Courtesy of Jamie Graziano

standard was created through a joint effort of a number of TICA judges and Old-Style Siamese/Thai breeders in North America. This breed is not recognized by the CFA.

GENERAL APPEARANCE: The ideal Thai/Siamese cat should be medium to slightly large and have pointed ears, resembling Thailand's indigenous pointed cats. The trademark of this breed is its apple-shaped face and, a distinctive, wedge-shaped muzzle.

HEAD: The Siamese cat's head should be long and taper into a wedge shape. The wedge should begin to taper from the ears, forming a triangle. The head should be medium-sized in proportion to the body. Allowance will be made for a stud cat.

SKULL: The skull should be flat. In profile, a long, straight line should easily be noted from the top of the head to the tip of the nose. There should be no bulge over the eyes and no dip in the nose.

EARS: The feline's ears should be slightly oversized and pointed, with a wide base.

NOSE: The nose should be long and straight, a natural extension of the forehead with no bulge or break.

MUZZLE: The feline should have a medium-long muzzle with a slight wedge shape that is rounded at the tip.

EYES: The Siamese cat's eyes should be medium to slightly large, with a gentle convex curve above the eyes. Round, almond-shaped eyes will be disqualified. Eye color should be blue, but unlike CFA guidelines, brilliance and luminosity are more important than depth of color.

CHIN and JAW: The chin and jaw should be neither weak nor prominent, and they should be aligned vertically with the nose.

NECK: The neck should be medium length.

LEGS: The feline's legs should be medium length, graceful in form, but not muscular.

PAWS: The Siamese cat should have an oval shape, medium size, in proportion to the cat.

TAIL: The tail should be as long as the torso, tapering gradually to the tip

COAT: The coat may be short, fine-textured, glossy, and lying against the feline's body.

CONDITION: The cat must be in good physical condition. Eyes should be clear and bright. Musculature should be firm, but lithe, not meaty or dense. When picked up, cats should weigh about as much as one would predict visually.

BODY: Preferably, the body should be a very pale off-white with the point trace color of the cat. Evenness of the body color and contrast with the points are more important than extreme whiteness. Point color should be dense and even. Mask, ears, feet, and tail should match in color.

TICA will allow incomplete color points and masks in kittens up to the age of twelve months. Darker body shading in older cats is allowed as long as there is still a definite contrast between body and points. However, felines will be disqualified for a visible tail fault or crossed eyes. Temperament should be unchallenging; any sign of a definite challenge shall be disqualified.

Show Life

Preparing your cat to become a show cat requires a lot of time, energy, money, care, and determination. Here are some things you should know about show cats:

Show cats are not easy to find – Show cats are not easy to come by, so do not expect to phone a breeder and request a show cat, especially if they have never met you. Show cats are the cream of the crop, and not every litter produces a show-cat quality kitten. Often, you will have to wait one year or more for a show cat. Some people wait years for a cat out of a specific litter.

Show cats have to remain intact – Show cats cannot be neutered or spayed. Often you do not have a say in the gender of your show cat. Show cats originally were designed to show off the breeding stock of the cat's bloodline. The cat's appearance and structure are judged according to the cat's ability to produce quality pedigree kittens.

Be prepared for co-ownership – The majority of breeders who agree to sell you a show cat often will retain partial ownership of the cat. Perhaps the breeder will want to maintain the breeding rights to the cat or to protect the bloodline and prevent the cat from being bred irresponsibly. Be sure to read the fine print on the contract before you sign.

Be determined to work – Show cats do not get in the ring and automatically strut their stuff. Your Siamese cat will need conformation classes to learn how to be handled by strangers, be properly socialized, and travel well.

Do not expect to get rich – Cat shows are not money makers; instead, they are quite expensive. However, if your cat places first, you will get bragging rights.

Preparing for the Show

Cat shows are nothing like dog shows. Instead of parading through an obstacle course with their felines, cat handlers sit in designated spots. The cats are often placed in cages with an assigned number. The judges observe each cat and judge according to each specific breed standard. A winner for each breed is chosen, and the winning cat moves on to the finals.

The best way to understand how to show your Siamese cat is to go to a cat show. You will have the opportunity to talk to cat handlers and ask for advice, get a feel for how things work and see how cats are judged. Here are some suggestions from expert Siamese handlers to prep your feline for a cat show:

Grooming

Be prepared to spend hours grooming your Siamese prior to a show. The majority of cat shows will require your cat's nails to be trimmed just before the show, so make sure to bring along a pair of nail trimmers. Generally, cats will be disqualified if their claws have not been recently clipped.

Vaccines

Most shows require that your cat be up to date with its vaccines so it will not put other entrants' health at risk. Be sure to bring along proof of your furry friend's most recent vaccines.

Membership

Cat shows are often sponsored by a number of different organizations, and sometimes they require you to become a member before you can enter your feline into their show. Do your research ahead of time, as each cat show has different regulations and requirements for entry.

Comfort

Invest in a good-quality cat crate for transporting your kitty to and from the show. Make sure your cat has enough room to stand up and turn around inside of the crate. The crate should have adequate ventilation. Avoid using disposable cardboard crates, as cats are known to escape from this type of carrier.

Practice

Get your cat used to being handled by a number of different people, such as men with deep voices or women with high-pitch voices. Once your cat is used to being around unfamiliar people, have your guests feel your cat's tail and try to open her mouth, as this is a common procedure for a judge at a show. Expose your cat to as many different situations and environments as possible while she is young to help her perform her best in future cat shows.

Curtains

Show curtains are essential for showing your cat. The curtains are designed to line the outside of your cat's cage, preventing her from seeing her adjoining neighbors and creating an atmosphere less conducive to

Photo Courtesy of Zelde Becker

verbal and physical alterations. Ideally, the curtains will be made to fit your cat's cage (the cage size will be included in the show announcement).

Curtains can also be used to accentuate your cat's natural beauty, such as deeper hues that match her eyes to accentuate her creamy body. Avoid using white or cream curtains, as these will make your Siamese cat appear washed out. Choose a material that is easy to clean and transport. If you do not have the time or money to make your own curtains, large bath towels with safety pins are permitted.

Other cage items

Consider your furry friend's personality and add any items to the crate that might make her feel at home — a favorite toy, a blanket, or an elevated shelf to lie on. The show will provide litter for your cat, but it may be wise to bring along a litter pan.

How Cat Shows Work

Each cat registered at the cat show will be presented to a judge by its owner. However, some pet owners prefer to hire a professional handler or exhibitor.

You must fill out the CFA official entry form for each cat you plan on entering in the show. The CFA form is available in PDF form or online.

Read over the rules for the show, as each show has its own rules and regulations, such as entry procedures, entry eligibility, and responsibilities of the exhibitors. The CFA establishes the standard for each breed, like color definitions and disqualifying features.

Some shows offer an early bird discount for the registration fee. All shows have a specified closing date for entries, so be sure to send your entry at least a week before this date. If you do not receive a confirmation of your entry application, call the entry clerk to verify that your cat is registered.

It is prudent to arrive at least an hour before the announced time of judging. When you arrive, you will meet an entry clerk at the entrance, who will give you a cage number and benching row destination. Set up the cage according to your cat's requirements. After that, check the judging schedule and locate each ring so you will not be late or miss your cat's class judging time.

The judging process requires a lot of time so take advantage of that during your cat's class to see the different breeds and chat with the feline owners. If your cat will be out of your sight, it is always recommended to ask your neighbor to keep an eye on your cat while you stroll around the show.

The sole purpose of a cat show is to evaluate the cat's breeding stock. Your Siamese will start off in classes competing for points toward her CFA championship. Your cat will win points according to the number of cats she defeats in the cat show. The more cats of the same breed that enter a competition, the more points a cat will win.

Each judge will give his or her own opinion as to which cat represents the CFA breed standard appropriately.

How to Find a Cat Show

Organizations such as CFA and TICA put on hundreds of different types of shows each year. In the USA, cat shows organized by the CFA are by far the most popular. Each year the CFA Cat Championship is held in Madison Square Garden. This is the cat version of the Westminster dog show, with more than 325 feline breeds competing. To find a cat show near you, look at the CFA and TICA's official web pages for an updated schedule.

CHAPTER 13

Common Hereditary Diseases and Illnesses for Siamese

All cats, whether purebred or mixed breed, are prone to diseases and abnormalities, which may be genetic. Your purebred Siamese cat is no exception.

Many of these health issues can be unapparent to the average person for years and can only be detected by a medical screening performed by a veterinarian.

Understanding some of the health problems that may affect your Siamese cat can help you take precautions to avoid future troubles. For example, if a certain cat breed has an inherent risk for dental issues, then precautions can be taken to regularly clean the cat's teeth and avoid sugary treats.

Common Hereditary Diseases and Illnesses for Siamese Cats

By purchasing your Siamese cat from a reputable breeder, you will be able to verify the health of at least up to three generations of your kitten's family health. However, if your kitty was adopted from a shelter, she most likely will not come with a pedigree ensuring a clean health background, so it will be even more useful to be aware of which breed-related health problems you should watch out for.

Gangliosidosis

Gangliosidosis is an inherited disorder of lipid metabolism, also known as lysosomal storage disease. Affected Siamese cats lack an enzyme to metabolize certain lipids (fats), causing the fats to accumulate within the cells of the body, causing an imbalance in normal cellular function. Affected cats develop progressive neurological symptoms, such as tremors, eye twitching, a lack of coordination while walking, stunted growth, and an enlarged liver.

The disease is evident in a kitten between one to five months of age and will progress to the point of extreme weakness in the front and hind legs. Affected kittens will die at eight to ten months of age. DNA tests are available to detect both carriers and affected cats with gangliosidosis. Unfortunately, there is no known cure for the condition.

Photo Courtesy of Linda A. Bremner

Niemann-Pick Disease

Niemann-Pick is a hereditary disease caused by a lack of the enzyme sphingomyelinase, resulting in an accumulation of this enzyme in the cells, nervous system, and internal organs, such as the liver, spleen, kidneys, lung, and intestines.

Clinical signs of this disease become apparent from three months of age, and symptoms may include uncoordinated walking, head tremors, loss of balance, muscle weakness, and splayed legs. Affected cats will die before one year of age. There is no known treatment. DNA tests are available to detect both carriers and affected cats.

Progressive Retinal Atrophy

Progressive retinal atrophy refers to a group of different degenerative diseases that affect a feline's vision. This disease causes the light-sensitive layers of cells inside of the eye, the retina, to slowly deteriorate over time, eventually leading to blindness. Retinal dysplasia is diagnosed in kittens around two to three months of age, and a later onset form is diagnosed in cats between the ages of four to nine years.

Progressive retinal atrophy is an inherited disease that occurs in a long list of breeds and mixed-breed cats. Affected cats should not be used in breeding. If a cat develops progressive retinal atrophy, its parents and all of its siblings from previous litters should be prevented from breeding. Unfortunately, there is no known cure for progressive retinal atrophy.

Polycystic Kidney Disease

Cats with polycystic kidney disease will have numerous liquid-filled cysts in their kidneys. These cysts eventually become so large or numerous that the cat's kidneys fail. Some early onset symptoms of this disease are poor appetite, frequent urination, increased thirst, weight loss, and lethargy.

Genetic testing is available for the mutation that causes polycystic kidney disease. Before purchasing your Siamese kitten, make sure that the kitten and both its parents have tested negative for this gene. Treatment involves a specialized diet, fluid therapy, and regular medication to reduce the buildup of cysts.

Asthma

Asthma can go by many names, such as feline bronchial disease, allergic bronchitis, and allergic airway disease. Siamese cats are by far the most affected feline breed, with the condition affecting up to 5 percent of all Siamese cats. Feline asthma cannot be cured, only treated. Asthma causes the feline's airways to the lungs to narrow or become inflamed. If you notice your cat develops a wheezing cough, be sure to get her to a vet as soon as possible. Both inhalers and oral medications can help control your furry friend's symptoms.

Photo Courtesy of Carrie Ann Gray

Cats commonly won't show any signs of early hip dysplasia and may never exhibit symptoms if the disease is mild. More severe instances of this condition may manifest the following symptoms:

- Trouble jumping
- Lameness or limping
- Muscle loss in rear limbs
- Irritability or lethargy

If you notice any of these changes, consult your veterinarian for examination, diagnosis, and treatment options. In addition, hip dysplasia can be hereditary, and breeders should screen for hip dysplasia in their breeding pairs.

Hip or Joint Dysplasia

Joint dysplasia is a deformity of the joint that occurs during growth. Joint dysplasia often occurs in the hip joint. During growth, the thigh bone and socket for the pelvis need to grow at the same speed. However, in joint dysplasia, this growth does not occur, resulting in a loose joint, which is followed by osteoarthritis or degenerative joint disease as the body tries to stabilize the loose joint.

Joint dysplasia is a genetic disease, but the extent of damage can be affected by diet, environment, exercise, growth rate, and hormones. Siamese cats are especially prone to hip dysplasia. Care should be taken to keep your cat at a healthy weight, especially during her growth cycle, by feeding her a healthy, balanced diet.

Glaucoma

Glaucoma is a painful eye condition that can affect Siamese cats. Glaucoma often begins in one eye, but eventually, it involves both eyes, leading to complete blindness. Even though this condition is very painful, cats do a good job of concealing their symptoms. Subtle signs of glaucoma may be a cat that is hiding, less affectionate than normal, and reduced grooming. More obvious signs of glaucoma in cats are a partially closed eye lid, swelling, pawing at the eyes, discharge, bloodshot eyes, dilated pupils, or temporary blindness.

Glaucoma causes increased pressure in the cat's eye caused by failure of the eye's drainage system. This increased pressure can eventually lead to the destruction of the cat's retina and optic disk, leading to permanent blindness. If diagnosed early, treatment may involve surgery and medications to reduce the eye pressure, preserve vision, and manage pain.

Mediastinal Lymphoma

Feline mediastinal lymphoma is associated with felines who were not vaccinated against the feline leukemia virus (FeLV), and it commonly occurs in younger Siamese cats. Mediastinal lymphoma develops within the chest cavity, often causing respiratory difficulties. Fluid often accumulates around the tumor, making it even more difficult for the feline to breathe.

Photo Courtesy of Emily Miller

Mediastinal lymphoma can be treated if discovered in time. With aggressive chemotherapy protocols, between 50 to 80 percent of cats will achieve complete remission within four to nine months of treatment. Ensure your kitten and her parents have all been vaccinated for FeLV, to avoid costly veterinarian treatments in the future.

Strabismus (Cross-eyed)

Convergent strabismus is the medical term for crossed eyes. Siamese cats are prone to this birth defect. If a cat is cross-eyed, its parents and all of its siblings from previous litters should be prevented from breeding. Unfortunately, there is no known cure for strabismus. Strabismus is not dangerous, and no treatment is needed. Most cross-eyed Siamese cat owners find this trait to be quite endearing.

Photo Courtesy of Cait & Del Burns

Other Common Diseases or Health Conditions

Not all diseases and health conditions are hereditary. Diet, lifestyle, and just plain bad luck are all factors that can affect your cat's long-term health.

Small Intestinal Adenocarcinoma

Siamese are predisposed to developing small intestinal adenocarcinomas. If your cat has a tumor of the small intestine, you may notice vomiting, reduced appetite, lethargy, and unexplained weight loss. The vomit may have a coffee-ground appearance, and stool may be black with a foul odor. Your veterinarian will be able to diagnose small intestinal adenocarcinomas and recommend an appropriate treatment.

Pica

Feline pica refers to when cats eat nonedible things with little to no nutritional value, such a s dirt, plastics, fabrics, rubber, plants, or paper. Pica is common in all cats, but especially in kittens. Untreated, this habit can cause serious health issues, as it can cause blockages in the cat's intestinal tract. This disorder may be caused by stress or other medical issues such as nutritional deficiencies or pancreatitis.

If you suspect your cat has pica, start by seeing your veterinarian, as they will look for any underlying medical conditions. Provide your cat with additional mental stimulation, so that she is not bored. Pick up any objects your cat should not be eating and place them out of her reach.

Feline Hyperesthesia Syndrome

Anesthesia means the lack of feeling or sensation, and hyperesthesia means the complete opposite — too much feeling or sensation. Siamese cats are prone to hyperesthesia.

Felines with this syndrome have increased sensitivity to touch that stimulates their nerves and skin. The feline's skin will often ripple along the back with even the lightest touch. Often an affected cat will cry, run away, or self-mutilate, trying to lick the pain away. Medications can relieve the cat's pain. Your vet will do several tests to rule out other medical issues.

CHAPTER 14

Caring for a Senior Siamese

Your Siamese cat has provided you with countless hours of love, laughs, and companionship over the years. Now that she is getting on in age, it is your time to repay all of her unconditional love with extra love and care to ensure her senior years are happy ones.

Physical and Mental Signs of Aging

Unfortunately, felines age faster than their pet owners. Some cats begin showing age-related mental and physical signs as early as seven or eight years, while others are still friskier than a kitten at ten years of age. A general rule of thumb is a Siamese cat is classified as a senior if she is ten years or older.

As a parent of an aging feline, you will want to watch for changes in behavior that may indicate an underlying medical issue. The more aware you are of typical signs of aging, the sooner you can make your cat's golden years more comfortable. Here are five common age-related symptoms you may observe in your senior kitty:

Sleeping all the time or not at all – Slowing down is perfectly normal as your cat ages, but if you notice your furry friend is sleeping all the time or snoozing more deeply than normal, it may indicate a serious health issue. On the other hand, a normally lethargic cat that suddenly has more energy may be suffering from hyperthyroidism.

Difficulty jumping or climbing stairs – Arthritis is common in senior cats. While your cat may not limp or show obvious signs of joint pain, you may notice she has difficulty jumping up onto the couch or into the litter box.

Unintentional weight loss or weight gain – Unintentional weight loss in an older cat, may be an indication of any number of problems, from heart and kidney disease to diabetes. On the opposite end of the spectrum, as your senior cat ages, her metabolism may slow down and may need extra calories than she used to. If you notice your Siamese cat packing on the pounds or if notice she losing weight unintentionally, it may be time to talk to your vet about transitioning to a senior cat food.

Behavioral changes – Is your Siamese cat having accidents when she never did before? Does she avoid human interaction? These may be an indication that your cat is in pain or is mentally confused. Talk to your vet to get to the bottom of your furry friend's behavioral changes.

Photo Courtesy of Toni McGowan

Photo Courtesy of Debora Williams

Matted or oily fur – A sign of a sick cat is a lack of self-grooming. Your cat may be taking a break from grooming herself due to pain caused by dental issues or arthritis.

Senior cats should regularly see a vet every six months. If you notice any change in your felines behavior, you should not hesitate to call sooner.

Your senior Siamese cat may also begin to display symptoms of cognitive decline, such as forgetting where her water dish is or simply meowing at nothing. Your cat may seem to be going senile, which is entirely possible as cats can develop cognitive problems just like humans. Many behavioral changes are caused by feline cognitive dysfunction syndrome (FCDS). FCDS is similar to Alzheimer's disease and affects around half of all cats over 14 years of age.

At around 15 years of age, almost 70 percent of all cats begin to experience symptoms associated with FCDS. Some behavioral changes your Siamese cats might display are

- House soiling
- Increased anxiety
- Fear of familiar people and objects
- Compulsive behaviors
- Excessive meowing and vocalization
- Change in activity level
- Insomnia, sleepwalking, or restlessness

If you observe your Siamese cat displaying any of these symptoms, consult with your vet. Your vet will make a diagnosis by asking you a few questions during the visit. There is no cure for FCDS; however, there are medications and therapeutic options, such as dietary therapy, nutritional supplements, and maintaining a healthy and stimulating environment.

Illness and Injury Prevention

> *Six-month vet visits are important after the age of 10 for your aging Siamese. Your vet will help you keep an eye on any changes in your cat's health. Siamese are known for teeth and kidney issues, and blood work will help identify those issues early. Beware of ketamine used as a pre-op for anesthesia. Breeders are not sure why, but our slinky breeds tend not to flush this out of their systems, and health issues can ensue.*
>
> JULIE ZWEMKE
> *Zelines*

Strained muscles, sprains, and pulled ligaments are all common senior feline injuries. As your Siamese cat ages, she will become more susceptible to injury due to brittle bones and arthritis. Research shows cats experience a similar pain threshold as humans. You can easily reduce injuries by incorporating the following strategies into your older cat's daily life:

Avoid extreme temperatures – Elderly Siamese cats are more sensitive to extreme temperature changes. Purchase an electric heating pad for your cat's blanket or place her blanket near a heat source at night. If your Siamese cat goes outside, keep in mind that she can suffer more easily from heatstroke, frostbite, and hypothermia than younger cats. If the weather outside is too hot or too cold, keep your kitty inside.

Daily exercise schedule – Even though your senior Siamese has gotten slower in the last few years, that does not mean she does not need regular exercise or mental stimulation. Play hide-and-seek with your cat, or play with her with a feather.

Ramp up – Climbing stairs or jumping up on the couch may become a challenge for your senior cat. At your local pet supply store, you can find a variety of ramps to help.

Slip-proof your home – Your Siamese cat may lack the agility she once had during her younger years. Your hardwood or tile floors may cause her to slip, causing injury. Place rugs in the areas your cat spends the majority of her time to help her feel more secure and sure-footed.

Soft, fluffy bed – Your Siamese cat will thank you for a soft, fluffy bed that supports her old bones and joints. Invest in a kitty bed with soft sides, so your senior kitten can rest her head on a soft surface while she observes her surroundings.

Take it slow – Your elderly Siamese cat will need extra time for eating, walking, going to the bathroom, etc. Be patient with her, and give her the time she needs. Your furry friend also will appreciate extra attention, love, and affection from you, like cuddling on the couch.

Weight control – Since your senior Siamese cat is less active, she is burning fewer calories, meaning unwanted weight gain. Extra weight puts pressure on your old cat's bones, joints, and heart, which can cause additional health problems. Consult your vet for recommendations to improve your cat's diet.

SIGNS OF ILLNESS OR PAIN

Any change in your Siamese cat's behavior may be an early indication that she is ill or in pain.

When your cat is in pain or is ill, her eating or drinking habits will often change. She might lose interest in food or drink excessive amounts of water. She may become withdrawn, be aggressive when petted, or seem unwilling to play with her favorite toy. Your cat may display one or more of these signs of ill health:

- Runny nose, crusty eyes, or discharge coming from the ears
- Excessive drooling
- Vomiting
- Diarrhea
- Constipation
- Difficulty urinating
- Coughing
- Hot spots, excessive scratching, or skin sores under her coat
- Limping, swelling, and lack of mobility

If you notice that your Siamese cat is displaying any of these symptoms for more than forty-eight hours, consult with your veterinarian.

Age-Related Diseases and Conditions in Siamese

> *Because Siamese are partly albino, they are temperature sensitive. What this means is that their points (face, feet, tail, and ears) are the coldest parts of their body. Limiting their time in the sun when young or old will help keep these cats healthy. As they age, they will darken, and their once ivory or cream bodies will look close to their point colors. Even though they are in their senior years, they will always be kittens at heart.*
>
> AMANDA WILLIAMS
> *AW Cattery*

During your cat's golden years, she may begin to experience age-associated illnesses and diseases. Many of these conditions can be treated if identified early, so be sure to consult with your vet immediately. The following health issues are commonly associated with geriatric Siamese cats.

Arthritis – Just like people, cats develop arthritis as they age. The most common type of arthritis in aging Siamese cats is osteoarthritis, also called degenerative joint disease. This condition affects the hips, knees, shoulders, and elbows. The changes in joints result in pain, stiffness, and lack of mobility. Osteoarthritis is progressive, meaning there is no cure, but there are many treatments, such as chiropractic, hydrotherapy, and acupuncture, which are known to slow the disease progression and ease joint pain.

Cancer – Unfortunately, cancer is common in older felines. Different types of cancer can cause a variety of symptoms. Often, symptoms may be dismissed as signs of aging, such as lethargy or a lack of appetite. As your Siamese ages, it is vital that she receive routine wellness screenings. Lab work, diagnostic imaging, and exams can pick up on anything that is unseen to the naked eye. The sooner the cancer is caught, the better the chances of your cat's survival.

Cataracts – Cataracts cause your Siamese cat's eye to lose transparency, causing them to appear cloudy. The cataract prevents light from passing through your cat's lens, blocking her vision. Most elderly cats who develop cataracts will not completely go blind, and they can adjust to their loss of vision. Your vet will need to diagnose the cause of the cataract before coming up with a treatment plan.

Photo Courtesy of Sabina Schuttevaer

Glaucoma –Your cat's eye is made up of a jelly-like substance called aqueous humor. This liquid is constantly being produced by the eye. Normally, the eye drains itself of the old fluid, but if this does not occur, then glaucoma happens. Glaucoma in cats can have one of many causes, so be sure to consult with your vet to find the correct treatment.

Watch out for the following symptoms of glaucoma in your Siamese cat:

- Cloudy cornea
- Continual blinking or squinting of the eye
- Pupil does not respond to light
- Pupils are a different size in each eye
- Increased sleeping

Diabetes – Siamese cats are prone to developing feline diabetes. Diabetes occurs when the pancreas stops producing normal amounts of insulin and may be caused by heredity, diet, obesity, and certain medications, such as steroids used for treating allergies. Diabetes can easily be regulated with insulin shots and a change in diet.

Incontinence – Age takes a toll on your cat's organs, muscles, and nerves, making it more challenging to hold her bladder and bowels the way she used to. Incontinence may be an indication of other health complications, so you will need your vet to rule out some other issues first. If the vet does not find any health problems have her wear a kitty diaper.

Kidney Disease – Kidney disease often develops slowly, starting off as renal insufficiency and progressing to full renal failure. Once this disease starts to progress, there is no cure. But if is caught in time, it can be successfully treated to slow the progression. Signs of kidney disease include increased thirst, frequent urination, lack of appetite, vomiting, and lethargy.

Lenticular Sclerosis – This condition is often confused with cataracts as it also causes the cat's eyes to form a white, cloudy reflection. Lenticular sclerosis, however, does not affect your Siamese cat's vision. But to be on the safe side, get your cat's eyes checked out by your vet.

Muscle Atrophy – Muscle atrophy is common in older felines as they become less active with age. This condition causes rear leg weakness, limping, ataxia, paw dragging, flabby muscles, and weight loss. Muscle atrophy can be caused by a number of conditions, such as arthritis, injury, and sore muscles from lack of exercise. Your vet will need to give your cat a check-up to diagnose the cause the muscle atrophy before treating her.

Grooming

Grooming is essential throughout your Siamese cat's life, but even more so as she gets older. After all, Siamese cats are avid self-groomers.

Grooming sessions are an excellent opportunity to observe any changes in your cat's overall health, as many underlying health issues are revealed through the health of the skin and coat. Fur can begin to thin, and skin irritation, new growths, or lumps may start to appear.

One of the best gifts you can give your aging Siamese cat is grooming her daily, as it keeps her looking and feeling her best. Plus, your furry friend will drink up the extra attention from you. Your cat is never too old to be pampered!

TIPS FOR GROOMING YOUR ELDERLY SIAMESE CAT

Before grooming your cat, carefully review the detailed information found in Chapter 11 of this book and take into consideration the following tips to adapt the process for your old friend. These tips can go a long way in ensuring your elderly cat will receive the level of care and respect she deserves.

Make grooming a pleasant experience – Pet your kitty as you brush her and give her plenty of verbal praise or cat treats throughout the entire process. Use a calm, soothing voice, and avoid aggressively holding or confining your cat. Sometimes, more frequent, shorter sessions are better for both the cat and you, resulting in less anxiety for both parties.

Watch for signs of discomfort – Your older cat will communicate her discomfort through body language or by vocalizing. If you notice your Siamese cat whimpering, squirming, or shivering, then you need to stop the grooming session. Let your cat take a short rest or find a more comfortable position. If your Siamese cat becomes agitated or stressed, then discontinue the session and continue another day.

Bathing – If you need to bathe your elderly Siamese cat, there are a few precautions you can take to ensure her well-being and comfort. When bathing your cat, place a non-skid mat in the bottom of the basin or tub to secure her footing. Make sure the water is warm enough that your Siamese is not shivering during the bath. Often, geriatric cats need a special shampoo to treat dry skin or other conditions.

After thoroughly rinsing out the shampoo, dry your cat with warm, fluffy towels. Before using the blow dryer, let your Siamese cat shake herself off. Never use the blow dryer on the hottest setting. Instead, use the cool setting.

Be sure to get your old cat as dry as possible, as water trapped close to the skin may cause hot spots.

Brushing – Before you start brushing your Siamese cat, inspect the brush to make sure it's in good condition. If the brush's teeth are bent or

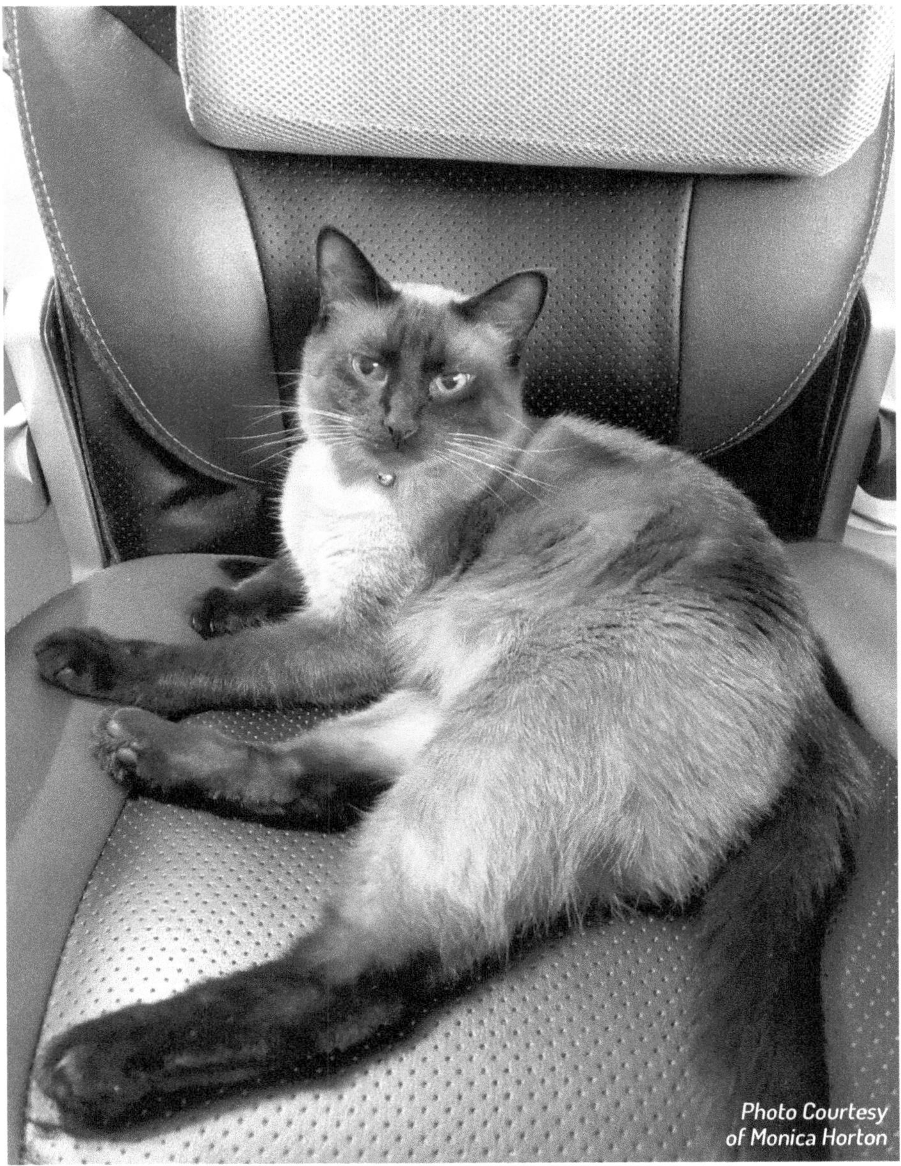

Photo Courtesy of Monica Horton

broken, it is best to discard it and get a new one, as the teeth can scratch an older cat's thin, vulnerable skin or damage her coat.

Arthritis and joint pain may make it difficult for your cat to stand in the same position for long periods of time. Place a blanket on the sofa and have your Siamese cat lie on her side while being brushed. Matted, tangled hair does not provide your cat with extra insulation as much as clean, tangle-free hair will.

While brushing your Siamese cat, be on the lookout for bare patches and brittle hair. This may be an indication of underlying health conditions. Also, use your fingers to feel for any new lumps, warts, or sores on your cat's skin. If you notice anything suspicious, consult with your vet.

Nail trimming – Your elderly Siamese cat will need her nails trimmed more frequently than when she was younger. If your old cat suffers from arthritis or joint problems, it is even more of a reason to keep her nails trimmed, as the nail length affects your cat's posture and can force her to torque her spine, causing additional discomfort.

WHY OLDER CATS STOP GROOMING

There are many reasons why your older Siamese cat might be grooming herself less. Older cats may find it physically uncomfortable to groom themselves. Many felines develop arthritis in their spine and hips, making the motions required to groom themselves very painful.

Arthritis can affect any joint, including knees, hips, elbows, spine, and toes. When a cat experiences pain while moving, it is unable to stretch its head to reach certain spots. Lack of grooming can cause increased dandruff, unkempt fur, mats, or a buildup of urine or fecal matter.

Many feline parents do not recognize their cats have arthritis, as cats tend to conceal their pain. Signs can be subtle, including:

- Getting up from a nap more slowly
- Decreased grooming
- Decreased activity
- Lethargy
- Litter box accidents

If you suspect your cat has arthritis, it is important to talk to your vet about supplements and pain medication that may help.

Nutrition Needs

Good-quality food is essential. In the older years, it may be necessary to go with a smaller kibble or add in soft canned food. Older Siamese who may have had dental issues where removal of their teeth was necessary can live a healthy, active life. They can still eat kibble but may require the addition of soft canned food as well.

KAREN SPOHN
Candi Dasa cattery

Your Siamese cat's nutritional needs will vary throughout her lifetime, and once she reaches her golden years, it can become a challenge to understand her new dietary needs. However, switching your cat's regular brand of cat food for a senior one may not be enough.

According to studies, once your cat reaches ten or twelve years of age, her caloric requirements may actually increase. Without enough calories and protein, your Siamese cat could lose muscle mass and become too skinny. On the other hand, your Siamese cat may tend to pack on the pounds, and you will need to decrease her daily caloric intake.

As your Siamese cat ages, her digestive system takes more time and effort to absorb the nutrients from her food, particularly fats and protein. Dental and digestive issues also mean your cat might find it hard to eat or chew the food she previously devoured, so maybe softer textures will be easier for her to eat.

Wet foods or those that increase your cat's water intake are also beneficial, as they aid in increasing the volume of urine your cat eliminates and lower the risk of urinary tract problems.

Another issue that may affect your cat's appetite is a decreased ability to smell and taste, so she may lose interest in her food. Your cat's food needs to be particularly palatable so that she will be more likely to eat it and continue to get the nutrients she requires.

Protein is vital for your Siamese cat's overall health. As your cat ages, she begins to lose muscle mass, even if she is still active. As her muscle mass is depleted, so are her protein reserves, causing her immune system to weaken. As your cat's immune system weakens, so does her ability to fight off infections and illnesses.

Your senior Siamese's diet should be made up of 60 to 80 percent protein. Avoid cat foods that contain fillers. Instead, opt for foods rich in lean red meats, fish, chicken, and dairy products. As always, check with your vet when monitoring your cat's weight and modifying her diet.

IF YOUR SENIOR SIAMESE CAT WILL NOT EAT

It is common for senior cats to lose interest in food. Try adding one to two tablespoons of bone broth or a small amount of canned food to entice your cat. If your elderly kitty refuses to eat for more than forty-eight hours, consult with your vet immediately to rule out any underlying health problems.

Bone broth is a stock made from simmering raw bones for several hours, either in your slowcooker or on low heat on your stove. This is a delicious, nutrient-dense superfood that will improve your Siamese cat's health and is guaranteed to get her to gobble up her dinner.

How to make bone broth for your Siamese cat:

Ingredients

- 4 pounds of raw bones with marrow (you can use chicken, turkey, rabbit, beef, or oxtail bones)
- 1/3 cup fresh parsley, chopped
- 3 stalks of celery, chopped
- 1/4 cup organic apple cider vinegar (helps to pull the marrow and minerals out of the bones)
- 6 to 7 quarts of water

1. Place all of the ingredients in a large pot or the slow cooker.
2. Cook on low heat for 8 to 12 hours on a low simmer or for 24 hours in a slow cooker on the lowest setting. Stir occasionally and add extra water if necessary.
3. Allow to cool. Remove the bones, celery, and parsley, and discard. Note that you should never feed cooked bones to your Siamese cat.
4. Once the broth is completely cool, place it in the refrigerator overnight. It will form a layer of fat on top, which can easily be skimmed off and discarded.
5. Freeze in small portions in Zip-lock baggies, then thaw before serving. Give your cat one to two tablespoons with each meal.

Choosing a Premium Senior Cat Food

All cats are obligate carnivores, which means the majority of their diet must come from animal protein. Here are some things to look for in a senior cat diet:

Highly digestible food – Digestibility is essential for proper nutrient absorption. Cats are designed to digest protein and not carbohydrates.

Plenty of protein – Research shows senior cats require a higher percentage of protein in their diet (at least 60 to 80 percent) than younger cats do.

Taurine – Taurine is an essential amino acid that is critical for your cat's cardiovascular health and is especially important for all senior cats. It can be found in animal-based proteins, such as chicken, lamb, beef, and fish. Any good-quality cat food will list taurine an ingredient.

Moisture – Senior cats often develop dental issues that make chewing hard kibble difficult. Wet food is easier for many elderly cats to chew and has increased moisture content that will be easily digested and improve kidney health. If your cat insists on dry kibble, try using a moisture-rich wet-food topper.

Sufficient calories – While senior dogs tend to gain weight as they slow down, aging cats have the opposite problem — they have trouble keeping the weight on. Work closely with your vet to determine the ideal weight for your senior cat. Then find the correct food and feeding schedule to help achieve and maintain that weight.

When choosing a senior cat food, it is important to consider your Siamese cat's individual needs and recognize that these needs can change over time. Just because one type of senior cat food is suitable for your furry friend now does not mean it will always be appropriate. Take your time to do your research and talk to your vet to find the best diet for your faithful companion.

Look for a senior cat food made from premium quality ingredients, such as human-grade organic lean red meats, free of artificial preservatives. No matter how healthy your Siamese cat is, there is no need to put a strain on her immune system by feeding her poor-quality, generic cat food with little to no nutritional value.

Transition your kitty slowly to a new senior cat food. It is best to start gradually by adding a small amount of the new food to her current food. Each day you can add a little more of the new food. Ideally, it should take seven to ten days to completely switch your cat to the new food.

Listen to your vet's recommendations, especially if your cat has been diagnosed with a condition such as diabetes, kidney, liver or heart disease, arthritis, etc. Your vet will most likely recommend a prescription diet. While these diets often do not include the word "senior" in the title, they are formulated to manage disease conditions commonly seen in elderly cats.

Saying Goodbye

The very thought of having to say goodbye to your four-pawed companion for the last time is beyond heart-wrenching.

Often, when we begin to observe signs that our cats are suffering and dying, we start to second guess ourselves or go into denial. This often causes our beloved felines to suffer far longer than they should have. The question is, how do you know? When is the right time to put your best friend into a forever sleep?

Telltale signs your Siamese cat is dying

Prolonged lethargy or disinterest – One of the most common signs of the dying process is finding your cat lying in the same spot (often not where she would normally rest), barely acknowledging you or other family members. Cats may become lethargic due to other health conditions, but if the veterinarian has ruled this out and the lethargy lasts for more than a few days, then maybe it is time to consider saying goodbye.

Stops eating or drinking – Another classic sign something is wrong with your Siamese cat is when you offer her the tastiest treat imaginable, and she refuses to even sniff it. Often at this point, the cat will stop drinking water, as her organs are starting to shut down. Try keeping your cat hydrated by giving her water using a dropper or turkey baster, but if she still refuses to swallow, there is not much you can do at this point. Be sure to rule out other health conditions with your vet.

Lack of coordination – The next sign is when your cat begins to lose balance and motor control. When your elderly Siamese tries to stand up, she may be very wobbly or disoriented. Or she could shake or convulse while lying down. In this case, make your cat as comfortable as possible and remove any objects she could knock over if she tries to stand up. Note: Saying goodbye to your cat means protecting her, creating a safe area for her, and providing whatever help she needs.

Incontinence – When a cat is dying, often, she will not even move from the spot to relieve herself, even if she has diarrhea. This is an indication that your cat's organs are starting to shut down. During this stage, make sure you keep your Siamese and her bed clean and dry.

Labored breathing – Toward the end, many cats display labored breathing. Your cat's breathing may become difficult, with lengthy gasps between each breath. This is an extremely hard moment, as you know that your cat is suffering.

In 2016, a 30-year-old Siamese cat named Scooter was dubbed the oldest living cat by the Guinness World Records. Scooter was born on March 26, 1986, and lived in Texas with his owner, Gail Floyd. The oldest cat ever documented was a 38-year-old cat from Texas named Crème Puff. Unfortunately, Scooter passed away only days after being awarded the title.

Seeking comfort – Despite your cat's quickly deteriorating health, she will look for comfort from her people — from you. During these final hours, be with your cat, reassuring her of your love and affection.

Making the decision

The signs above are not always consistent and will vary, as some cats suddenly pass away in their sleep without any indications of ill health. Part of preparing to say farewell to your Siamese cat is realizing you may have to make the difficult decision for your cat by intervening. Before making a decision, talk over all of your options with your family and come to a mutual agreement.

Once you have come to the decision to intervene to end your cat's suffering, discuss the options with your vet.

Veterinarians are required to follow a set of guidelines called the "Humane Euthanasia Protocol," whether the euthanasia is performed inside of the clinic or in the tranquility of your own house. The entire process is painless and stress-free for your Siamese cat. The Humane Euthanasia Protocol is considered the kindest way to put your cat to sleep.

The Humane Euthanasia Protocol:

1. The veterinarian will inject your Siamese cat with a pain tranquilizer.
2. Once your cat is relaxed and sedated, then your vet will insert an IV to administer the euthanasia solution.

3. The vet will leave you alone with your cat for a few minutes for any final goodbyes, then return to administer the final drug to stop your Siamese cat's heart.

Certain North American veterinarians are not required by law to adhere to the Humane Euthanasia Protocol. Instead, they practice a quicker and more affordable method to stop the animal's heart with a single injection of barbiturates. Barbiturates cause the animal's central nervous system to slow down, causing a painful death. This type of euthanasia is not humane, as it is not pain-free, causing the animal short-term distress and anxiety.

Ensure your veterinarian agrees to apply the Humane Euthanasia Protocol to your cat. If not, look for another veterinarian who will.

Most cats are euthanized inside the veterinary clinic, but many vets will make house calls. If your vet is unable to make house calls, you can find an extensive list of reputable veterinarians throughout the United States and Canada online at the In-Home Pet Euthanasia Directory. (www.inhomepe-teuthanasia.com)

Here is a quick overview of the pros and cons of getting your Siamese cat euthanized at home versus at the clinic.

At-home euthanasia may be the right choice for you if:

- Your Siamese cat is too sick to be transported comfortably to the veterinary clinic.
- You personally feel more comfortable grieving at home.
- Car trips or visits to the veterinary clinic cause your cat anxiety and stress.
- Money is not an issue, as at-home procedures cost more.

Vet clinic euthanasia may be the right choice for you if:

- You want your usual vet to perform the procedure, but they are unable to perform house calls.
- You prefer a more neutral environment for the procedure.
- Your cat is still mobile enough to be comfortably transported in your car.
- Cost is a concern.

Whether you decide on euthanasia at home or at the veterinary clinic is a very personal decision. There is no right or wrong answer.

The cost of clinical euthanasia can be between $80 to $350, depending on where you live. The cost of at-home euthanasia can cost between $300 to $800. The higher cost may include add-ons, such as cremations, funeral services, or getting the vet to take an impression of your cat's paw to cast into a memento.

It is highly recommended you pay for the euthanasia before the procedure as emotions can be running high when the procedure is final, and the last thing you need is to relive the heartbreak by receiving the bill later. When it is all over, you can request the veterinary clinic to dispose of your cat for an extra cost. Some clinics offer cremation or a professional burial service at a nearby pet cemetery.

Take your time grieving your Siamese cat and coming to terms with your loss. Everybody does it in their own way. Saying goodbye to your Siamese cat does not mean forgetting about her. With time, you may start thinking about opening up your heart to another cat.

"How lucky am I to have something that makes saying goodbye so hard."

Winnie the Pooh

CPSIA information can be obtained
at www.ICGtesting.com
Printed in the USA
LVHW070843181222
735465LV00001B/8

9 781954 288539